Spirits of the Fire

Jaq D Hawkins

Illustrated by Jeremy Scott

Spirits of the Fire

©1999 Jaq D Hawkins

ISBN 186163 076 X

ALL RIGHTS RESERVED

No part of this publication may be reproduced, stored in a retrieval system or transmitted in any form or by any means, electronic, mechanical, photocopying, scanning, recording or otherwise without the prior written permission of the author and the publisher.

Cover design by Paul Mason
Internal illustrations by Jeremy Scott
Cover painting by Marc Potts

Published by:

Capall Bann Publishing
Freshfields
Chieveley
Berks
RG20 8TF

Acknowledgments

Thanks are due to my daughter and friends who support my efforts in writing these books, and to all the fiery people in my life who have inspired me, upset me, and shown me in various ways the value of taking action.

Special thanks go to Kevin Bullimore for setting me on my way toward this series, and to Sandy Brock for her help with information on Caballah.

Dedicated to my own Fire child, Wendy LeFay

The Author

Jaq D. Hawkins began magical study as a child and has been aware of elemental spirits from a very young age, despite a primarily urban upbringing. Her writings on various aspects of magical theory are recognized in American as well as British occult magazines and are repeated on various computer networks. Her writings on the relationship of elemental spirits to the natural laws of our world are unique to this series of books. Ms. Hawkins currently lives in the North of England with her daughter.

The Illustrator

Jeremy Scott is a native of North Yorkshire where he attended Harrogate College of Arts. He has sold his artwork in private galleries as well as doing commissioned work, primarily his astoundingly realistic technical drawings. More recently, he has also become known for his striking landscapes. He has diversified his talents into designing theatre sets, illustrating children's books, and has even turned his hand to specialized interior design in San Francisco. His special talent for incorporating elemental creatures into his drawings is a valuable asset to this series.

Also By The Author:

Understanding Chaos Magic
Spirits of the Earth
Spirits of the Air

Books In Progress;

Spirits of the Water
Spirits of the Aether
The Chaos Monkey

Table of Contents

Introduction to the Spirits of the Elements Series		9
Chapter 1	The Nature of Fire	13
Chapter 2	Types of Fire Spirits	21
Chapter 3	Dancing With the Fire	31
Chapter 4	Places to Find Fire Spirits	41
Chapter 5	To See Fire Spirits	51
	To Seek Fire Spirits in Nature	53
	To Seek Fire Spirits in the Home	57
	Spontaneous Sightings	58
	To See Invited Fire Spirits	59
Chapter 6	Fire Spirits in Natural Magic	61
	Folk Magic	63
	A Hearth Spell	64
	Reaching Into The Spirit of Fire	66
Chapter 7	Fire Spirits in Ritual	71
	Calling Quarters	73
	Outdoor Fire Rituals	76
	Fire Spirits For a Specific Task	76
Chapter 8	Fire Correspondences	79
	The Tree of Life of the Caballah	81
	Incense Correspondences	84
	Planetary Rulerships for Incense Making	85
	Numerology	87
Chapter 9	Fire Thought-Forms	91
	Creating a Fire Thought-Form	95
	Sustaining a Fire Thought-Form	97
Chapter 10	Divination With Fire Spirits	99
	Invoking Guidance From Fire Spirits	102
	Keeping a Fire Divination Spirit	104
Chapter 11	Living With Fire Spirits	107
Appendix		110

Introduction to the Spirits of the Elements Series

The *Spirits of the Elements* Series began when a friend of mine who is a palmist told me in a reading that I was destined to write a series of books about nature spirits. At first, I tried to associate this prediction with a series of children's books which I was working on at the time, as it involves characters and events taken directly from my studies about elemental spirits. However, my friend insisted that this was not the series of which he spoke. There would be a series of books written for an adult audience which he was looking forward to reading.

At first, I wondered if the material would have been sufficiently covered by books already in print. However, this concern melted away as the chapters began to form in my mind.

I believe in fairies. Call them what you will, I believe that the spirits of natural things, and some things which would seem at first as not natural, exist whether or not we choose to believe in them. These elemental spirits are very much a part of our world which we cannot afford to ignore or dismiss if we are to understand our own magical nature, or that which draws us into the world of magic.

The four alchemical elements are Earth, Air, Fire and Water. References to these four elements are used in many forms of

Paganism and Magic. They represent the material world for Earth, inspiration for Air, determination for Fire, and emotion for Water. There is a fifth element called Aether. This represents Spirit.

In the following chapters, I will explain the associations and correspondences which humans have attached to the element for this volume, but let's not forget that this is essentially a book about nature spirits. It is their nature that I hope to express in these pages. I also hope to offer some practical information about the methods of perceiving these spirits and perhaps inviting them into the home or into ritual practices. One must remember that these entities cannot be commanded, only invited. I strongly recommend respecting their independence. It is no accident that old tales about fairies often warn of danger, or at least trickery! More about that later.

One quick note for those who wish to see fairies; visual perception is rare but not unknown. They are not physically perceived with the eye in the same way as solid objects. If one studies the medical information learned over many years about how the eye perceives line and colour, one learns that there are receptors in the eyeball called rods and cones. The rods, which are shaped as the name would suggest, perceive line and definition while the cones, which are shaped like little round cones (what a surprise) perceive colour. The combined messages are sent to the brain and we 'see' things as a whole comprising defined shape and colour.

Seeing nature spirits requires a shift in our perception because the rods in our eyes perceive nothing from them. It is the cones which can perceive nature spirits, which is why they are so often depicted as brightly coloured and fanciful little creatures. To an extent, their shape is defined by what we expect it to be. It is also because they are perceived with the cones that they become elusive when one tries to look directly at them. Cones perceive periphially. To see a fairy, one must try to catch it with the corner of one's eye. Perhaps this is at least part of the reason that so many people find it difficult to believe that they were ever there at all...

Chapter 1

The Nature of Fire

Fire is the element of action, of passion, of transmutation and of change (preferably in accordance with Will). Fire is the element of inner ecstacy, which cannot be adequately described to someone who has never known it. Fire rules all forms of magic, because magic is a process of change. Sexuality and passion, the sacred fire of sex, the spark of divinity which shines within all living things are all associated with the element of Fire. Yet the intensity of passion which lies behind the spirit of Fire far transcends the basic primal urges which initiate reproduction. To quote William Shakespeare; "Love is only one of many passions."

The passion of Fire encompasses all that represents drive, life force, progression, fortitude, and the inner experience of the Divine Fire of spiritual inspiration as well as sexuality in both its base and spiritual forms and the exigency of desire in all its guises. Where Air represents intellectual inspiration, Fire represents the spark of action which brings the inspiration into manifestation.

Fire is often symbolized by the Sun. It is depicted in churches with sunburst images to represent the Fire of God. Many religious texts speak of inner experience of the Fire, or of the Divine Light. During the Crusades, the Christians imported symbols for the Islamic Fire and incorporated the Persian Ahura Mazda into their own version of God, which also carries influences from Babylonian, Assyrian and Sumerian Sun cults.

Fire is also symbolized as light, which in its turn is provided by the Sun as well as the spiritual light which is spoken of in the *Tibetan Book of the Dead*. Shamanic religions believe that at death, the soul inhabits a spiritual body which preserves the Fire, or the light of being. At birth, the soul is given the 'spark' of life as its material beginning. Conversely, the Buddhist Nirvana is described as 'blowing out the Fire of desire'.

On a practical level, Fire provides heat, light and the ability to cook, but can also bring total devastation if uncontrolled. Here on planet Earth, the Sun is the source of light and warmth. It is the originator and generator of life. Without it, we would die. It is no wonder that the Sun in some form of representation is central to most forms of religion.

Practicality and folklore come together in many traditions and even in superstitions regarding Fire. In crofting communities, one of the accepted duties of the woman of the house (traditional keeper of the continuity of the family) was to get up in the morning to bring the Fire back to life and to meditate on the hearth and home. This is a form of folkmagic which still survives in some remote communities. The lighting of bonfires on hilltops has historically been used as an early warning system during times of war in Britain, yet is also associated with Fire festivals such as Midsummer and Lugnassah (*Laa Lunys* in Manx). Leaping over a Fire is an old fertility rite, as is the driving of cattle between two fires which is also a purifying ritual. Christian women less than a century ago still kept a consecrated candle burning during and after the birth of a child until the infant was baptised to keep the fairies from stealing it, which was connected to the underworld associations of Fire as well as the Christian belief that fairies were lost souls of the dead or fallen angels. On the Isle of Man, it is considered unlucky to lend Fire or even tinder and flint on New Year's Day, or sometimes on the 6th of January which is an older date for the New Year.

Spells which involve energy, authority, sex, healing, destruction, purification, or spiritual evolution are associated with Fire.

Fire is the reformative element, as in the Fire from whence the Phoenix rises again and again. It is also the element of consummation and purpose. Fire continues until all resources are exhausted. Fire is a powerful element, which can be used for positive or negative results, and one which can easily get out of hand if not carefully contained. Fire magic can be frightening, yet fear can be a powerful tool in magic. Fire magic may be used in divination, love spells, healing, protection, purification and many other uses, but should always be handled with caution.

Spirits of Fire come in more forms than one might guess. The most obvious is the spirit of a flame, whether it is a small candle flame or that of a raging forest Fire, but there are also the possessive spirits of passion and Will, the Spirit of The Dance, spirits of hot places, of light, and of chemical reaction. Fire spirits have purpose, and they continue so long as there is fuel for that purpose. Fire never just gives up.

A Fire spirit does not necessarily have to take form in flame, but may well perform its purpose in the realm of Spirit, existing on the very edges of physical ignition. The spirit of Fire can be summoned through the most primal forms of magic; drumming or dance for example, which easily lead to ecstatic trance. Fire has many underworld associations including most underworld gods and goddesses. The worship of some of these old gods has historically been connected to the act of animal and human sacrifice, which is one of the reasons why many modern Pagans shy away from Fire magic.

An efficiently constructed bonfire

Yet the principle of life force magic works in many ways, and leaving behind the barbaric customs of another age does not separate us from access to this very potent spiritual force.

Understanding the spirit of Fire lies in learning to understand our own human passions and drives, and in this understanding lies the key to learning to contain the spirits of Fire. Just as we learn from when we are children to control our primal drives and actions in order to operate within the bounds of social acceptability, we are able to learn to contain the spirits of Fire within parameters, once we understand their basic nature.

Fire magic is often performed using a flame in one form or another, yet can also be performed through ecstatic passion, sex, dance, or even the stirring of strong, sometimes negative, emotions. Fire is the driving force behind Spirit. It is the force which inspires us to carry on despite obstacles and delays, or to pursue that which may seem unobtainable.

Keeping the Fire under control lies in understanding its basic nature every bit as much as a firefighter understands the principles of the behaviour of flames. As is true with all of nature's elements, Fire behaves chaotically, but within the confines of physical laws which may be understood.

Fire spirits are living spirits. Just as the more commonly perceived Earth spirits live within plants and rocks, Fire spirits live within the potential for flame. This potential reaches far beyond the flame itself, and includes Fire spirits which exist totally in the world of Spirit. Sometimes these Fire spirits can possess our own human spirit for a time. Like Air spirits, Fire spirits can be insubstantial.

In magic, the Fire element is often invoked for purposes of action. Fire spells may be used for purposes for which other spells have proven insufficiently powerful or active. If the purpose is important enough, the magician will brave the obvious dangers.

I am very aware of the fact that many of my writings on magic are riddled with warnings and cautions. One might expect that a book which focuses on the element of Fire may contain little else. Not so. Although there is always a need for caution and circumspection when using magic of any kind, I will not hesitate to encourage the reader to embrace the power of Fire.

As I said earlier, aspects of divinity invoked for Fire spells are often associated with the underworld in some form. The mystery of Fire is associated not only with passion, but also with the mysteries of death. This is yet another reason for circumspection when dealing with spirits of Fire, and yet the mysteries of the cycle of life and death are integral to the most basic magical philosophies.

The focus of a Fire spirit ritual may be a flame of a candle, campfire, hearthfire or bonfire, but the habitat of the spirit lies in Spirit; in the infinite potential which knows no time or space. The realm of a flame spirit lies just beyond the level of manifestation. Any Fire safety official can confirm that Fire can ignite suddenly in the right conditions, the flames erupting spontaneously from the potential of heat and fuel. In a similar manner, a Fire spirit can spontaneously manifest as a burst of flame, as an action or even as a burst of illumination. This illumination is different than the inspiration which may be brought about by an Air spirit; it is a sudden awakening of knowledge of the mysteries. This is the basis of all religious ecstasies.

Fire spirits are often depicted in art as demons or inhabitants of subterranean underworld communities. Cartoons show us little flames with mischievous expressions on their fiery faces, spreading their kind prolifically in the scene, or as little demonic creatures from the Christian mythologies, which multiply rapidly and inundate the situation to the chagrin of a main character who is suffering the consequences of incaution. This sort of depiction is not as fictional as their creators may intend. Fire spreads easily, the Fire spirits giving rise to many more of their kind so long as there is fuel to feed upon. Yet it can be contained.

Fire is primarily associated with passion and the life force, and also with anger. Both anger and passion are strong emotions, both are difficult to control. Both are powerful tools in magic, as the Fire spirits attracted or created by these emotions are as strong as the emotions themselves, and are not as easily squelched as a visible flame. Yet they are independent spirits, apart from human creation every bit as much as the spirit of a candle flame is apart from the human who struck the match.

Fire is a cleansing and purifying force, as well as a driving force. Creation and destruction exist within the same potential, within the erratic mood shifts which characterize the spirits of Fire. Fire is transmutative. The same force which can create terrifying destruction in a building Fire can melt sand into pure, clear glass. It can destroy infection as efficiently as it can destroy a forest. From destruction comes new life, as depicted by the Phoenix. From the flames of purifying transmutation comes the gold of alchemy. From the chemical reaction in a nuclear explosion comes wanton destruction, yet from the smaller explosion of Air and fuel in the combustion engine comes the power of machines.

In nature, Fire will periodically cleanse a part of the Earth such as when lightning strikes and begins a forest Fire, yet from the wake of destruction will grow new life. In the red hot heat of lava which pours over the Earth are the nutrients which enrich soil to grow especially healthy crops. In our fear of the destructive nature of Fire, we sometimes forget the

Phoenix, we sometimes forget that in the wake of destruction comes new potential. We fear the transmutation. Yet therein lies the value of knowing the spirits of the Fire. What is magic, if not transmutation?

The worship of Fire gods has all too often focused on the destructive principle historically. Our society has evolved sufficiently now to see the balance in creation and destruction, to focus our efforts on that which we wish to create and to destroy only to clear the way for this creative intent.

The energy of Fire is a consumptive force. It cleanses by consuming relentlessly until there is nothing left to consume. The wise magician will remember this. Just as a campfire will be fed by a predetermined supply of wood, a Fire spell should have its resources predetermined and set aside, material or spiritual, so that the spell does not get out of control and consume the life force of the magician. The destructive force of Fire can lead to death, yet the creative spirit of passion and drive leads to life and continuity. Fortitude and perseverance are fuelled by Fire. Fire draws energy into itself. The ancient Celtic shamans used this principle when kindling the Needfire.

In understanding the spirits which we associate with Fire, we learn to understand the eternal balance of creation and destruction, which is often depicted in legend as the age old battle between good and what is perceived as evil, or the Sun god and his adversary. When we understand the natural balance of these things and the essential need of one for the other, then we can understand the nature of the spirits of the creative, the destructive, the transmutative and driving force which we know as Fire.

Chapter 2

Types of Fire Spirits

"Did the Fire look at you?"
--Donald Sutherland in *Backdraft*

One might think of Fire spirits as being of a kind; little spirits of flame which inhabit every sort of flame from that of a candle to a raging Fire. Indeed there are attendant spirits of this sort of Fire, just as many Earth spirits are the attendant spirits of the growing things in nature. These are certainly the most obvious form of Fire spirits, but there are more varieties than one may at first imagine. One might also expect that spirits which can be associated with Fire in myth and legend are likely to be demonic depictions, and the demons of Christian mythology should certainly be included in the folkloric list, but there are also less negative associations of Fire spirits in this category. They appear less frequently than with any of the other elements, but they are certainly present.

Fire associations occur in many, sometimes subtle, forms. The fairy horses of the Tuatha De Danaan for example are made of fire and flame, not of dull heavy Earth, and are therefore reputed to be as fast as a brush Fire wafted by a heavy wind. They have a broad chest, large eyes which reflect Fire, and quivering nostrils. Such an intimidating presence is easily associated with the element of Fire.

The observant reader may have noticed by now that I have included mention of the Tuatha De Danaan in *Spirits of the Earth*, *Spirits of the Air* and now of their horses here in *Spirits of the Fire*. As I have explained in the previous volumes of this series, elemental associations with spirits are to an extent a matter of human perception, except in cases where the spirits are very much of the actual element, and more than one association may attach to a spirit form. Given that interpretations of many traditional elemental spirits may vary from one person to another, we can only attempt to classify them as best we can by their origins and characteristics. In the end, how we interpret mythological or traditional folkloric spirits is largely an individual matter. It is only when dealing directly with living elemental spirits, such as during magical operations, that understanding their actual nature becomes very important.

Some other examples of traditional Fire spirits are as follows;

FIREPLACE FOLLETTI (Italian)
These hypnotise young brides with their burning eyes, which fills them with melancholy and despair.

FEE (French)
Sometimes called Fates (Fétes). A general term for fairies in French, but they were associated with fertility originally, and fertility results from sexual passion which is associated with Fire. The Fee should not be stopped from borrowing things, which they do frequently, and are dangerous to dance with. An unwary human who is caught into their whirlwinds of dance will die of exhaustion.

TYLWYTH TEG (Welsh)
Dancing fairies who live underground (underworld associations) and wear bright colours, chiefly red. They come forth on moonlit nights and dance in circles, sometimes

enticing unwary travellers into their dance where they play tricks on them. Also called Verry Volk in Gower.

RARASH (East European)
This spirit lives on a farm and appears as a hen or small boy. It is associated with the hearthfire. It brings gifts to the farmer stolen from neighbours.

SALAMANDER (multi-cultural)
The salamander is the Fire form recognized by most Wiccan religions in ritual, but is also associated with Fire in other cultures. Salamanders are desert creatures in the flesh, and are age old representatives of underworld Fire. This is partially a serpent association, and is also a result of the fact that most salamanders live in deserts and hide under rocks to escape the hot Sun.

BASILISC (Western European, French)
The Basilisc is a mythological creature with a glance powerful enough to kill a man. One legend claims that it was created by an alchemist, from the alchemical Fire. It lives in the vicinity of springs and fountains, which might suggest a Water spirit connection, but I include it with Fire because of the alchemical association.

VOUIVRE (French)
A snake-elf. It appears beside fountains, has a diamond in its forehead which protects it, and which is kept out of sight while drinking or bathing. A man who captures the diamond will gain tremendous power and wisdom. Robbed of its treasure, the Vouivre will pine away and die. Again, we have a serpent association with a spirit which lives near Water. There are many examples of Fire spirits who live close to Water, which one can presume is a natural control over the rampant nature of Fire as an element.

DRAKE (English, German, French, Scandinavian)
These travel through the Air as a flaming ball or fiery stripe, but are a house spirit. They develop an intense relationship with the master of the house and bring gifts of gold and grain. In return, the master must provide gifts of food and reverence. To insult the Drake endangers the existence of the house it lives in. They smell of sulphur, and it is considered wise to get under cover when they pass. They can take a variety of shapes and forms, and are also known by the names Grak or Drachen, as well as Fire-Drakes.

DRAGON (multi-cultural)
Dragons come in many forms, most of which are associated with Fire. Dragons and serpents are an archetype which represents the cycle of creation and destruction, and the Kundalini spirit of sex and magic. There are a few exceptions to the direct Fire association such as sea serpents, but again we find a dual nature in such creatures, as the intensity of Fire lives in the spirit of such a creature, even when it lives in the sea. The Fire-breathing dragons of fairy tales are probably the first association to occur when dragons are mentioned, unless the reader is of Chinese ancestry or is very familiar with Chinese culture. Chinese dragons are generally a more benevolent form of this particular archetype, yet are still depicted as fierce creatures with large sharp teeth.

LAMIA (Greek)
In Greek mythology, the mother of some illegitimate children of Zeus who are slain by Hera. She mates with a dragon and is a bad housekeeper. Apparently Zeus got around a bit as there are more than one Lamia. They appear as large, uncouth women and slay children in revenge for the loss of their own.

INCUBUS/SUCCUBUS (Multicultural)
A seductive spirit which comes to humans at night to copulate. The incubus is a male spirit, the succubus a female.

They tend to heterosexuality. Old legends claim that they bring nightmares, but this is likely an interpretation decided by a sexually repressed society. Incubi and succubi respond to the lust of human need or desire.

JINN (Arabic)
Properly called jinnee, jinneeyeh for the female, anglicised to genie. The Jinn may be good or evil. They are very long-lived, have magical powers and are formed from Fire without smoke. They can mate with humans and produce offspring which will have the attributes of both.

As in the previous volumes of this series, I have included only a few samples in the list of folkloric elemental spirits. Forms of these spirits are known in different cultures by many different names, and there are any number of traditional spirits which could be looked upon as Fire spirits by human definition. Apart from the obvious flame spirits, the most common archetypal Fire spirits are a varied selection of serpent forms. As explained under 'Dragon' above, there are many images from different cultures for serpent symbols. In many cases, there is also an association with Water. The serpent is representative of kundalini in Tantra, which in turn associates the serpent with sex magic.

Serpentine patterns occur in nature in such things as the course of a river and the spiral energies in Earth magic. They occur in man-made sacred sites like the Great Serpent Mound in Ohio (see *Spirits of the Earth*) and a dragon temple in Cambodia which is designed to correlate its buildings to the stars in the constellation Draco. Sometimes the serpentine association is with a worm, and there are legends in various parts of the world about actual wormlike or serpentine creatures which are occasionally seen by humans.

The most well known of these is the Loch Ness Monster, but another interesting case is the Mongolian Death Worm. This is a large worm-creature which reportedly lives in the sands of the Gobi desert, swimming through its sandy ocean as though it were a serpent in the sea. It suddenly bursts forth through the dunes to attack its victims, usually camels, which it kills with an electric charge or poison. The locals call it the Orgoi Horhoi. Those who claim to have seen it say that the camels can smell it and will react to the danger just before its appearance. Like many such creatures, it has never been photographed or proven to actually exist, but there are enough individual sightings, as well as dead camels, to merit attention. This creature, real or not, has become part of the folklore of the region and is believed by some to be a demonic sort of spirit. The Mongolian shamen believe that the spirit attacks those who are a threat to their nation, but that it attacks in dreams. Oddly, there have been injuries on explorers who have investigated the sightings, after having had vivid dreams of the creature. Its appearances most often seem to occur in areas where a particular poisonous plant called 'goiho' grows.

Spontaneous sightings of Fire spirits in the wild are less common than those of the other three basic elements, yet they do happen and are all the more memorable for their rarity. Magicians and firefighters are most likely to encounter them, for very different reasons.

Fire spirits in art are mostly limited to cartoons, yet there are exceptional paintings which depict Fire spirits either in possession of their element or in human/spirit form such as the occasional succubus, usually in religious paintings. In films, demonic Fire spirits haunt the celluloid of many old black and white "B" movies and lustful demons attack the unwary in more modern colour horror films. This all gives rather a nasty connotation to Fire spirits through this medium, which may be a bit unfair. The only film I have personally seen which hints at the genuine nature of Fire spirits is *Backdraft*. In this film about firefighters and the nature of the beast which they continually encounter, there are subtle references to an intelligence behind the Fire itself, as is cryptically uttered by an imprisoned arsonist in the quote at the beginning of this chapter.

An important point to remember about Fire spirits, and particularly about flame spirits, is that the Fire follows its own physical laws and patterns, but it does so because it is the Fire. It destroys because that is what it does. There is no personal malice, only a continual consumption by a powerful element which is free of controls for a time. It is the task of the firefighters to regain control. Not to destroy the beast, only to stop that portion of it which has been unleashed. Having accomplished that goal, all of the humans involved will continue to live symbiotic lives where Fire, under controls, is very much a needed element in their existence.

Invoking Fire spirits can significantly increase the potential for Fire to get out of control, sometimes without an obvious physical connection. Several years ago, at a Pagan event in Scotland, there was an incident where a caravan on the site caught Fire for no apparent reason. Luckily nobody was hurt, but the caravan and its contents were completely destroyed. Many people will have put it down to coincidence, but there was quite a lot of Fire related activity involved in this event, including fireworks and firewalking. One wonders if perhaps a more balanced programme of events might have been a good idea.

As I explained in the first chapter of this volume, Fire spirits exist just beyond the material level of ignition and can be easily attracted or enticed to manifest. This is a useful thing to remember in a situation where one is trying to light a match, perhaps for a campfire, or an incense coal which is a bit old and not cooperating very well. A quick invitation to the spirits of Fire can make all the difference, which I can personally attest to. However, this aspect of Fire spirits should also be borne in mind in situations such as the calamity at the event described above.

On a material level, the spirit of a large fire is no different in essence than the spirit of a candle flame, just as a spirit of a small pebble is really no different than the spirit of a large boulder (as explained in *Spirits of the Earth*). The source of fuel determines the material lifespan of the Fire spirit. The spirit in the sparks which emanate from a sudden electrical charge exist only for a moment like an Air spirit which exists for the moment of a breeze, while a candle flame spirit will continue for as long as the candle burns.

In theory at least, the qualities of these spirits also apply to other forms of Fire spirits. However, there is a marked difference in the form of manifestation of other sorts of Fire spirits, particularly possessive spirits.

The spirit of passion is a possessive spirit, that is, it is an actual spirit which temporarily possesses a human host, usually by invitation (or at least implied invitation). Possession can be a touchy subject, due to films like The Exorcist and the Christian perception of possession. However, giving oneself over to temporary possession is a well-established practice in forms of magic which pre-date christianity. Some methods of ritual or divination involve such possessions and are generally accepted, but the fact that possession is involved is often forgotten. Channelling is one example, which is adapted from an older form of mediumship. Ecstatic dance is another. These practices go so far back in history that no one really knows when they were first practised, and survive in various forms today, sometimes even as the latest new age fads. They involve opening oneself up intentionally to spirit possession, but not in the way that nasty demonic creatures are depicted in horror novels and some of the more fanatical religious literature.

We do not always realize that we invite spirits into us. Like Air spirits, the Fire spirit potential is ever present and waiting for such an invitation, but like a Fire, the invitation can be contained and the resources controlled. The spirit is sent forth at the end of a ritual to perform its purpose, or disseminated at the completion of its task. The Fire spirit returns to the realm of spirit to await a new opportunity to manifest, in whatever form it might.

These are very powerful spirits who operate by the laws of nature. Their potential is not to be used haphazardly, but need to be contained within parameters which a competent magician can set. Christian mythology fears 'demons' because these laws of nature are not taught as a part of the religion, and any attempt by the ignorant to deal with nature spirits of any kind carries the potential for disaster. Fire spirits in particular have dangerous potential, yet possession by a Fire spirit through ecstatic dance or certain other methods which will be discussed in the appropriate chapters of this book naturally contains and directs the power of this element and the potentially destructive nature of the spirits of Fire.

Whether one works with possessive Fire spirits, potential or manifest flame spirits, kundalini or even the Fire spirits of legend and mythology, the laws of nature are much the same. Fire spirits are intense and impersonal, and the wise magician will respect their destructive potential. Yet no magic is as invigorating as Fire magic, and the spirits of this element are exuberant rather than malicious. It is for the magician to consider appropriate containment when s/he decides to 'dance with the Fire'.

Chapter 3

Dancing With the Fire

*"Oh, for a muse of fire,
That would ascend the
brightest heaven of invention."*

--William Shakespeare
Henry V

The steady rhythm of a basic drum beat pounds through the otherwise still night air. Soon, more drums join in creating new rhythms. The flames of the bonfire dance with the pure joy of being...intense, potentially creative as well as destructive. A mood is forming among the inhabitants of the place, and some begin to sway in the beginning rhythms of dance. They feel the need to move, almost as though they are being taken over by a spirit created through the sound and vibration of the drums, spurred on by the spirit of the bonfire.

As the dance continues, the spirit takes over and the dancing becomes wild, abandoned...the participants completely giving themselves over to the spirit of the dance. The scientists would quote brain enzymes as the cause, but there is something more. Something which science cannot adequately explain. The dancers are possessed by the need to move in rhythm..to express their passion through the dance. It is very much like the passionate spirit which possesses those who are

caught up in sexual passion. This, in fact, is very much the same sort of possessive Fire spirit. A spirit of nature which can possess the human drives and take form through the human body and spirit, as its brother Fire spirit takes form through the flame of the bonfire. Although the human has the power to break free of this possessive spirit, for the moment, the wanton abandon freely expressed in the dance is too joyful to forsake in the interest of control.

This Fire spirit, the spirit which possesses for a time, is every bit as much an independent entity as the spirit in the flame. Fire spirits are pack creatures; they give rise to more of their kind. Had the drummers played without the bonfire, the formation of possessive Fire spirits would have taken much more time and effort. It is the spirit of the bonfire which directs the dancers, probably unconsciously. The possessive Fire spirits dance with the pure joy of the central Fire, and with the passion which characterizes the element of Fire.

Dance inspires something in the human spirit which goes far beyond the explanations of science. Dance holds the rule of number, rhythm and order and as such, is a demonstration of the microcosm of the greater macrocosm of the universe. Many philosophers and creative geniuses in history have used dance symbology, including Nietzsche and Havelock Ellis. Yeats, in *A Vision*, uses the dancer to represent Unity of Being. Einstein was inspired by Russian ballet, Wagner praised Beethoven's 7th Symphony as "the apotheosis of the dance". Dance inspires not only creative genius, but creation itself. Austin Osman Spare states in *The Focus of Life* that "Only the animal in man dances...", yet there is much more of Spirit in the dance than the animal totems which are most obvious, and where there is Spirit, there is magic.

Fairies have long been associated with wild dances, particularly at night. Many fairy legends speak of men who are enticed into joining the revels of the 'wee folk', only to learn later that they have been dancing for more than a year without stopping (in the way of time differential in faeryland) or to drop dead from exhaustion because they are unable to stop dancing.

One form of magic which has been used by most primitive societies is to 'dance out' the wish. Humankind has traditionally acted out planting and harvesting to entice the gods to help crops grow. Tribal cultures express rituals of their beliefs through dance. In some cases, aboriginal cultures have acted out weather magic in relation to their needs, acting out the fall of rain or the growth of grain. Dance has also been used for telling stories which are passed down in this manner from one generation to the next. This practice has developed in modern culture into other story-telling dances such as the ballet and various forms of modern dance.

Another purpose for dance in tribal culture is to dance out intent for war, or to affect the hunt. This is a form of sympathetic magic which links tribal societies to some forms of Eastern mysticism.

Dance is a natural means of inducing mystical states and even trance. In Southern India, the caste known as 'Devil Dancers' dance through spinning and leaping in order to reach the degree of inspiration which is considered essential to their healing powers. A similar practice is used by Mongolian shamen, who dance to frighten away the devils of disease who afflict their tribesmen. Ecstatic dance is integral to the Bogomiles of Russia as well as the 'Dancing Dervishes' of Turkey, who are well known for their spinning dances which instigate frenzy and a deep trance state. Many forms of religious hysteria are achieved through wild dancing. It is a universal method for stirring up religious excitement practiced in some form in all cultures of the world. Some forms of these dances include an invitation to the gods to descend spiritually in the midst of their dancing worshippers.

Others are specifically used to incite the worshippers toward some action or to bring a magical attribute into the lives of the people. Fertility dances in particular are characterized by delirium and frenzy.

One significant feature of dance magic is that the ritual is most often contained within the dance, requiring no additional accoutrements for their practice. Rhythmic motions accompany not only primitive religious dance, but is apparent in the swaying of the body in more conservative and modern forms of prayer. Movement brings a form of comfort to the human soul, as is demonstrated by the gentle rocking which characterizes not only an upset child, but adults as well. It brings a feeling of self-healing. In her article, *The Power of Dance: Health and Healing* (The Journal of Alternative and Complementary Medicine, Vol. 1 No. 4, 1995) Judith Lynne Hanna, Ph.D tells us that, "*Dance may promote wellness by strengthening the immune system through muscular action and physiological processes. Dance conditions an individual to moderate, eliminate, or avoid tension, chronic fatigue, and other disabling conditions that result from the effect of stress.*" She goes on to tell us that dance involves the simultaneous use of right and left brain in an intricate sensory combination of movement, rhythm and music which uses most if not all of the senses. Dance may reduce or even eliminate pain. For some people, it provides a feeling of control that minimizes the sense of helplessness and fear which is related to pain. Dance involves the body, emotion, and mind simultaneously. People who dance regularly have been known to experience withdrawal symptoms if they are forced to stop for a time, including nervousness, headache and depression.

Dance is used to induce the temporary insanity of the Bacchic or Dionysiac rites, which include outbursts of savage violence. Witch doctors of some African tribes engage in a form of dance to "smell out" their victims. These dances awake the full

Dancing with the fire

potency of nature in the same way as the agricultural gods are aroused for growing grains. The history of magical dance is known as far back as the ancient Egyptian culture, and probably predates that in tribal societies throughout human history. It is a way of acting out the drama of the gods.

Indeed a similar form of sympathetic magic is aroused through Greek drama. The ancient Greeks used gesture to represent feeling, passion and action both in drama and in religious dances associated with the cults of Apollo and Dionysis. Dance is at the heart of many ancient mysteries. Lucian says in his *Peri Orcheseos* that "there is not a single ancient mystery in which there is not dancing. Those who reveal the ancient mysteries dance them out." The Geranos, or Crane Dance, is said to have been originally performed by Theseus on his return from the Labyrinth at Crete, which was danced at the festival to Apollo in the isle of Delos. The complex patterns of movement within the dance are supposed to represent the windings of the celebrated maze at Knossos.

Watching a dance performance brings out the immitative urge. We imitate their actions when watching someone else dance, our muscles twitching and flexing in sympathy with the performer's movements. We watch the dance and follow with the mind, seeing ourselves dance in the performer's place. To concentrate the force of intention in this manner is very much a part of the magic. As I said above, Fire is a form of spirit which gives rise to more of its kind. We are drawn into the performance, just as tribal peoples are drawn into the magic as they watch the dancers among themselves performing their rituals. The spirit of Fire draws all within itself, consuming with passion even as the Fire itself consumes its fuel.

Dance is closely associated with masking, often becoming a process of totemism or a connection between the living and the dead. It is used as preparation for the hunt or to

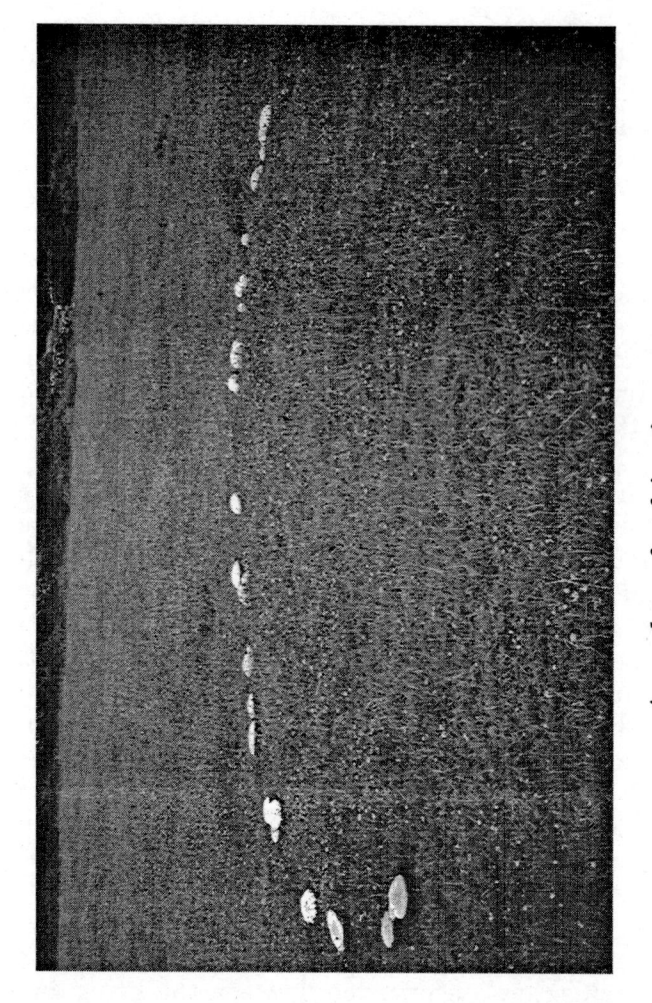

A nearly perfect fairy ring

commune with the gods, also represented by masked performers. The Corroboree of the Australian aborigines for example paint their bodies with stripes resembling skeletons to represent the dead. In this culture, only the men dance for ceremonies such as initiation, conclusion of peace and purely social functions. Dance has been used to accompany sacrifice in many cultures, such as among the Khonds of Bengal and Madras.

Ancient ritual dances survive today in folk dances of many cultures. All medieval folk dances, according to Canon MacCulloch, were survivals of Pagan ritual dances. The most important relic of the dances of the Middle Ages is the Morris dance. The exact origin of Morris dancing is not known, but the word 'Morris' is believed by some to be derived from "Moorish", which is one theory which would account for the black-face paint used in some forms of Morris dance. There is an alternative theory that it may be related to the coal industry from the Midlands of Britain, the black make-up representing the soot on the miner's faces.

Sword dancing appears in teutonic as well as Celtic folk dance, not to mention many Eastern and Polynesian traditional dances. Lewis Spence associated sword dances generally with war dances performed in honour of a deity of strife before going out to battle, which has obvious Fire associations. The Longsword Dance which occurs in the Morris tradition has definite Sun associations, as is seen when the swords, locked together, are raised to show the Sun-ray image created by the interlocking swords. It is the Fire of the Sun, the warmth, which induces the food of the Earth to grow. As I have said several times in this series, the elements in nature work symbiotically. Each of them plays an essential part, and the element of Fire is what gives drive to the forces of life which we see manifested often in the Earth element.

Some ancient Irish dances, often danced round bonfires, had a serpentine nature to them, although the association tends to be more in keeping with Water serpents than with the Fire association usually associated with snakes and serpents. One example is the *Rinke Teampuill*, or 'Dance of the Temple' which was performed from left to right, but changed if a horn was blown to indicate unfavourable omens.

The list of cultural and historic dances could go on and on, but all of these dances are brought together with a single form of spirit; a spirit of Fire which possesses and guides the dancer and the dance, the onlookers as well as the flames. It is through the dance that this spirit brings us as close as can be to experiencing the intensity of the Fire spirits in the fairy realm, like the Tylwyth Teg who dance in grassy fields. Dance is magic in pure spirit form. It is alive, it is intense, and it is free. It is a spirit of Fire which can be raised anytime, and in any place.

Chapter 4

Places to Find Fire Spirits

One might speculate that a place to find a Fire spirit is obvious, in a flame. It is true that flames, large or small, will certainly be attended by a gestalt Fire spirit, but there is more to Fire than just flame, as the reader may have begun to notice in the previous chapters of this book.

Anywhere where there is heat will be attended by at least the potential for a Fire spirit. This includes deserts, volcanic areas (especially in the interior of an active volcano) and places as common as a warm room. These places would be more prone to actual fires if the conditions were right, i.e. heat + fuel + oxygen = Fire, as any Fire safety official can tell you. It is within the heat element of this combination where the Fire spirit potential waits, ever patiently seeking the addition of the other two elements in order to spark forth into life. For this to happen, the heat must reach a sufficient level to ignite the available fuel, yet in the simplicity of the warmth lies the Fire spirit potential, always waiting in a state of somnolent consciousness.

Places where Fire tends to occur will also be watched over by a perpetually reincarnating Fire spirit. This includes such places as repeatedly used candle wicks, the hearth, bonfire sites which are used periodically and even your kitchen cooker. As Fire is frequently created in these places, the

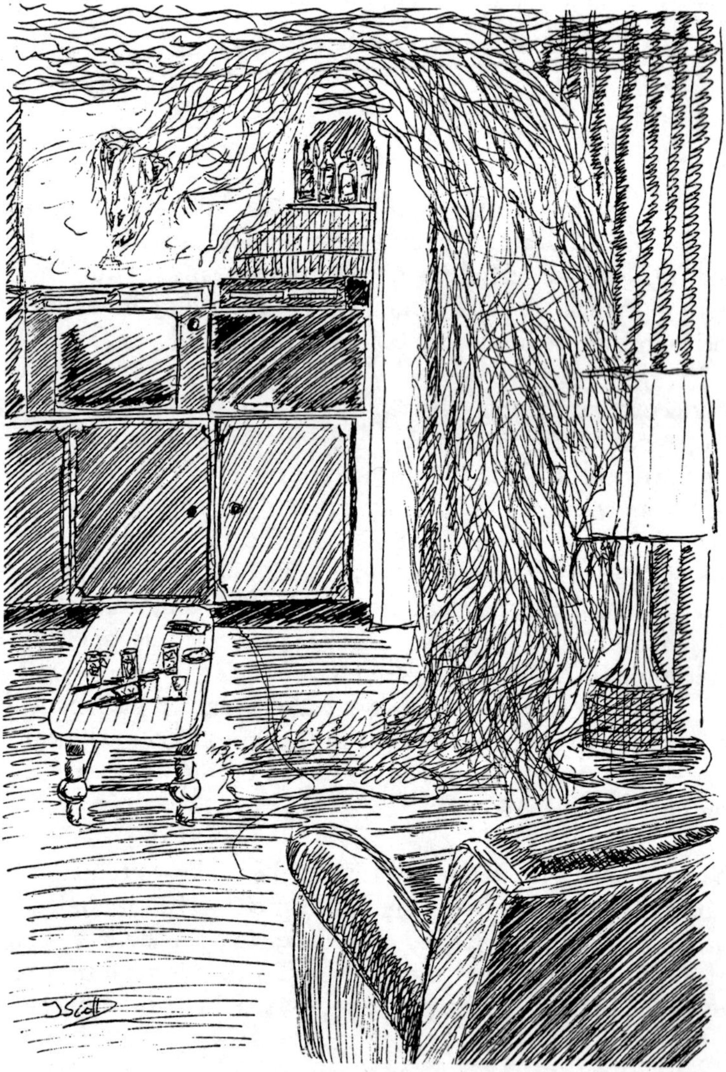

location itself develops an attendant Fire spirit which traverses between the state of potential and actual flame spirit as the Fire is lit and extinguished over time. Like a spirit of a place of Earth, these spirits become associated with their location as caretakers of the flame, ever renewed.

Like other elemental spirits, these place spirits are generally made up of a gestalt of many Fire spirits which come together in a common cause, that of giving the Fire perpetual life. This is particularly true of larger Fires, such as the Hearth Fire which is forever changing in size and intensity, never quite the same from one moment to the next, yet still existing as a continual Fire until it is allowed to fade from lack of fuel, only to be rekindled again and again.

Such a gestalt spirit can form for a bonfire as well if the same location is often used. These place spirits affect the 'feel' or spirit of a place, just as Earth and Air spirits create a specific feeling of a place within their own elements. A place where a Fire is repeatedly kindled in this way will become a place with a more intense feeling to it than those places where another element predominates. To an extent, a tension is formed between the Earth and Fire spirits because of the potential destruction if the Fire should get out of control, while a more playful feeding energy emerges between the Air and Fire spirits. The combination of these various energies can be electrifying, or terrifying. A ritual space where a bonfire occurs regularly very quickly attunes to the tribal instincts among attendant humans, bringing out the need for rhythmic music and The Dance.

The connection between the Fire element and the act of Dance is inherent. Dancing stirs up a spirit of passion within the human spirit. Not necessarily sexual passion, but something which lies far deeper in the soul. Dance has the potential for strong magic, and places where Dance regularly occurs maintain this spiritual energy. In the sacred space mentioned above, this becomes an important part of the overall gestalt Fire spirit of the location. In a place such as a theatrical stage, it is the focal energy of Fire spirit. This is a strong spiritual energy which translates to the members of an audience as a feeling of excitement and anticipation. This electrifying energy is almost visibly perceptible even to the most mundane attendee of the theatre on entering the room, long before the actual performance ever begins.

This sort of place spirit of Fire can affect a location long after the dancing has stopped. To the more spiritually aware person, it is not difficult to sense which stone monuments have a history of Pagan dance rituals, as the residual Fire energies still exist within the stones themselves, affecting the Earth spirit of the actual stone(s).

This general rule of Fire spirit locations also applies to places where sexual passion is frequently expressed. This may apply to a common bedroom, a brothel, or any place else where this energy is expressed on a regular basis. In the 1950's when premarital sex was socially stigmatized, teenagers used to find regular 'parking spots' where different levels of sexual activity occurred. Many of these places (those which have escaped the ravages of property developers) still attract couples who are either lacking a place of privacy or are simply feeling adventurous and perhaps a bit 'naughty' enough to conduct their liaison in a semi-public place. The energy of past sexual encounters often clings to such places, especially if they are relatively unchanged over time, and this residual association can stir a similar response from new visitors to the location.

Any place where strong emotions have been repeatedly expressed is likely to maintain an intensity which is associated with Fire in its location spirit. This includes places of ancient sacrifice (animal or human), such as the Coliseum in Rome for example which has been described as having an intimidating energy. Places which inspire with strong positive emotions are also influenced by an attendant Fire spirit, such as Mount Olympus which is traditionally the divine abode of the Greek gods, but is also the meeting place for the beginning of the modern day Olympic games. This place where the spirit of competition is continually renewed has been described as having a positive, uplifting energy. Whether the human spirit is stirred by the excitement of anticipation or with fear of the unknown, the location spirit which inspires these emotions is likely to be a Fire spirit. In the case of Mount Olympus, this spirit is allowed to take form in flame through the Olympic torch, but the existence of a Fire spirit is not dependent on actual flame.

Unlike Earth spirits, Fire spirits are not disrupted from a place when changes occur and cannot be extracted by removing the element. This is partly because Fire spirits live in their potential state most of the time rather than existing only in manifestation. The world of Spirit is generally invisible to the human eye, which is easy to forget when we seek glimpses of nature spirits or hear of so many occurrences of visible spiritual encounters.

Some places become associated with Fire through natural phenomena, such as places which have been struck by lightning. The oak tree is sacred to the Celts because it attracts lightning. Places with volcanic activity resulting in natural hot springs or geysers inspired awe from peoples in history, and still capture the imaginations of modern visitors. The La Brea tar pits in Los Angeles are still a major tourist attraction, and even inspired a fairly recent film, *Volcano*, which depicted the formation of a volcano by way of a lava fissure from beneath the hot tar which is a remote geological possibility. These places of natural heat or attraction of electrical activity have their attendant Fire spirits, along with whatever other nature spirits may inhabit the trees, rocks, pools or other features of nature which may be present.

A fire altar

Understanding the nature of Fire spirits helps to keep them within reasonable control in places where one might wish to create a contained Fire. A Fire spirit which is invited into the roaring flame of a bonfire in order to become guardian of a sacred place or into a candle flame for ritual purposes is more likely to remain within the intended confined parameters of its intended space than one which is left unregarded or taken for granted. The spirit will already inhabit the flames, but the invitation serves to strengthen the contact between human and spirit and to make a connection, rather like a friendship, between human spirit and nature spirit. This alliance serves to help maintain boundaries of expression.

More than the usual amount of caution is required when dealing with Fire spirits in a location, as their natural drive to consume can easily lead them out of control. Containing the space may not be sufficient, Fire can jump. Fire can spontaneously combust. Fire has a fierce desire to live and expand. This is where forming a relationship with the spirit of the Fire can make so much difference. A closely attended Fire is less likely to make any attempt to spread out of control.

A Fire can be encouraged to consume in such a way that purifies, such as rubbish burning Fires, and can double as a ritual Fire. As I have mentioned earlier, Fire is a traditional purifier in folk magic. Some modern people feel that rubbish should not be thrown on a ritual bonfire as it would show disrespect, but in my experience the Fire spirit responds favourably to being 'fed', regardless of the importance of the item which is offered. An empty cigarette packet is fuel to the Fire every bit as much as a sacred log. It will be devoured hungrily and the Fire will grow stronger for a moment as it consumes the fast-burning 'rubbish'. It is not offended, and the landscape is better off for the 'purification'.

Fire is an infinitely mutable element. It can be used for destruction, purification, change, and some forms of creation. A Fire spirit which is attuned to a cooker or campfire can be employed to infuse food with Fire energies while cooking, which can be done as part of a ritual or simply as a regular observance.

Caution is advised when doing rituals over a cooking Fire though. Cooking Fires can all too easily get out of control in any circumstances and invoking Fire spirits during the process can get out of hand. The reader is also advised to avoid places like gardens or dense forests for Fire rituals, unless a very well defined space is cleared and contained for the purpose. Fire is excitable, and a Fire spirit which is stimulated through ritual can, without any malicious intent whatsoever, extend itself beyond its intended parameters and create a very real burning hazard. As I explained in *Spirits of the Earth*, the resident Earth spirits are unlikely to appreciate having their abodes destroyed by flames which have got out of control.

Wherever Fire spirits are to be found, they can be perceived by the excitement and intensity which they inspire within our own human spirit. We are more closely related to spirits of Fire than many of us realize. Fire, as an element, holds the spark of life. Our bodies may be of the Earth, but the spirit which gives us drive and fortitude to live despite hardships and obstacles is of Fire. Flame is visible where Spirit usually is not, but the spirit of Fire which we perceive through dance (performed or observed) is much like the spirit we feel from a ritual round a bonfire.

The spirits of Fire take many forms, some of them are visible through flames, others can only be perceived psychically or through our own intense emotional responses. The spirits of Fire, in their state of potential, are with us always and can all too easily manifest anywhere if the right conditions should exist. But while there is need for caution when dealing with Fire, there is also potential for wonderful accomplishment. Fire keeps both of its edges very sharp.

The spirits of Fire are more strongly felt than seen, and places which contain them are easily distinguishable from those which are attended only by Earth, Air and/or Water spirits. Learning to recognize the different 'feel' of a Fire spirit comes easily to anyone with the most minimal sensitivity. It comes as a feeling of energy or power which inspires the stronger emotions, either in an uplifting response or one of alarm. Both extremes are very much of Fire. Both responses can be mastered with recognition. The spirits of Fire can be embraced with understanding rather than feared for their destructive potential. Remember that destruction is nature's process for renewal. All destruction leads to new potential as a forest destroyed by raging Fire soon begins anew with fresh, new seedlings.

It is human nature to fear the unknown, and therefore the key to embracing the Fire is to know it. We can learn to know Fire and to recognize individual Fire spirits with whom we share our existence. We feel their presence, we see their actions, we can learn their patterns of behaviour, and in some instances, we may even be able to see the Fire spirits themselves.

50

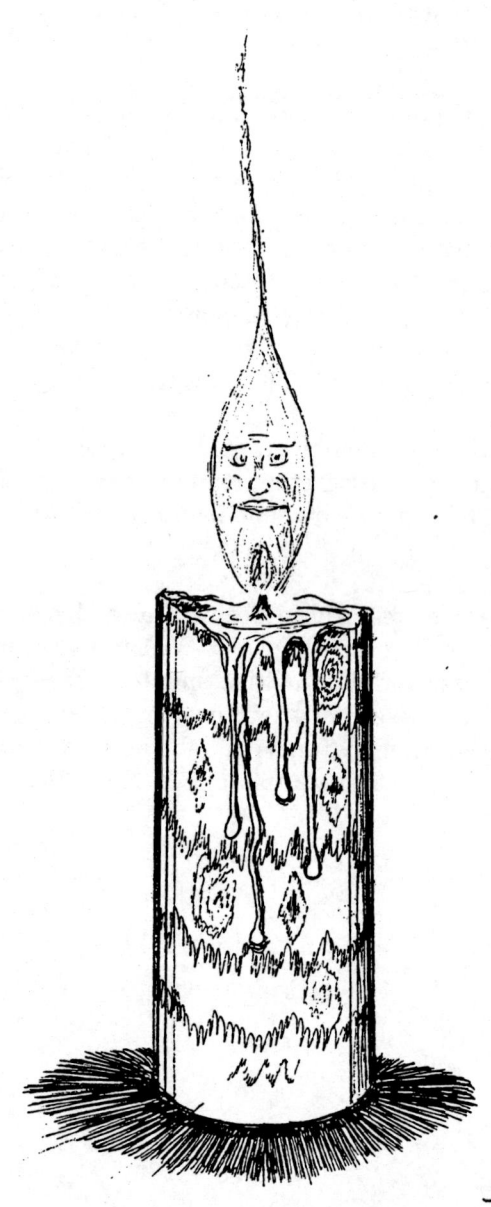

Chapter 5

To See Fire Spirits

To see elemental spirits of any kind is a tricky business at the best of times. In the case of Fire spirits, the most 'visible' are likely to be spirits of flames of one sort or another, yet there are exceptions to this.

I recently had a letter from my sister in Australia who mentioned seeing "small naked black men in a friend's garden", which she later learned was the site of an ancient aboriginal initiation centre. One can presume that these initiations involved ritual dance, and I would speculate that what she saw were residual Fire spirits who were created as a result of the ceremonies on the site. These ceremonies would have stirred excitement and life forces which are of the Fire element, yet they would not be dangerous as a Fire hazard as a life force spirit does not manifest in flame.

Correct or not, the supposition that these little men were Fire spirits is really not very far fetched, as spontaneous sightings of elemental spirits happen more frequently than most people realize. We just don't hear about them often because many people don't speak about them, assuming that they would be ridiculed for claiming to see 'fairies'.

The peripheral vision which is required to perceive elemental spirits can be deceivingly clear on occasion, and yet if one tries to look too hard or to follow spiritual beings they will most often seem to disappear very suddenly. It is our own concentration on them which takes us away from peripheral viewing, and therefore makes it impossible to see them any longer.

This should be borne in mind when attempting to see flame spirits, as should be the possible damage which could occur to the eyes if one stares intently into a Fire or even a small candle flame. Once again, properly perceiving elemental spirits becomes more possible when unfocusing vision.

This is one of the reasons why one is more likely to see visions in a Fire when the mind is allowed to wander rather than concentrating. Fire is the element of action. Fire spirits dance within the flame, acting out visions of the future as well as the present and the past, and the art of firegazing is very much a matter of learning to communicate with the spirit of the flame and also learning to look above, around, or through the flame itself without fixing the eyes on the potentially damaging Fire.

As most readers will know, one of the most basic practices in magic is the use of imagination and visualization. A firegazer will allow the imagination to wander while gazing at the area around a Fire and flitting the eyes about in response to images which, at first, may seem to elude definition. However, as the concentration is unconsciously drawn into the images which are created, they begin to take form. Some of them can be difficult to interpret, others form distinct pictures or symbols. It is very common to observe activity, perhaps even clear images of known people doing things which can be verified as a present occurrence or future event. This comes easily to some people, but may take a great deal of practice for others. Much depends on the ability of the firegazer to relax into the trance, which is what happens as the attention is drawn deeper and deeper into the images, or on the particular way that the mind of the firegazer interprets symbols. One friend of mine (who is an artist, and therefore very visually oriented) often sees images of fairy caves and other intricate patterns within the flame. Others may observe images of actual events.

The spirit of the Fire may well play a part in the pictures which are presented. As I explained in another chapter, flame spirits are particularly agreeable when it comes to communicating with human observers. The changing nature of the element of flame gives plenty of scope for the imagination to formulate images of the spirit itself, or for the spirit to present itself in a form of its own choosing. Of course other forms of Fire spirits can be observed besides flame spirits, as in the example described above. These spirits of Fire are not always of a kind which is likely to become flammable, but one should always be cautious when seeking them just the same, whether it is in nature or in the home.

To Seek Fire Spirits in Nature

Fire spirits in nature may be of several sorts. As explained in my sister's experience earlier, one form in which they may appear could be as resident spirits of ancient or modern ritual dance sites who can appear without warning. There is no reason for their manifestation, they simply exist as other Fire spirits exist for the sake of existence itself. They are residual energies which watch over the place where they were given form. If one should choose to dance with them, they can be easily revived to their full power and inspired toward some form of action through the dance. The method for attempting to see this sort of Fire spirit is much like looking for Earth spirits using the peripheral vision, but by looking for movement rather than a spirit which may be attached to an object. It is just a bit different when seeking visual perception of a possessive dance spirit. The spirit is still perceived through peripheral vision, but is seen sort of between the movements of the dancer(s). This sort of spirit is unlikely to run across your garden unexpectedly, but arises during the dance and disappears into its potential state soon after the dancing stops. However, repeated dance in the same location can eventually change the nature of the possessive spirit and give it external form. As with nature spirits of any kind, these Fire spirits can behave independently and in general I would recommend leaving them to their own business.

Some Fire spirits in nature can be terrifying, such as the spirits of uncontrolled Fires. The bystander who encounters such a spirit may well be in danger from the Fire itself, which is not a situation I would advise seeking out. On the other hand, if one is caught in an unexpected crisis situation, communing with the Fire spirit could possibly convince the Fire to pass you by, or to allow you through. Stranger things have happened. Again I stress that such a situation should never be sought out in order to 'test' oneself. Fire spirits are erratic, and may not be interested in your experiment or problems. There are no guarantees.

People who fight Fires for a living are in a position to meet Fire spirits on a regular basis. A psychic firefighter has an advantage over his or her comrades in that s/he can 'know' the Fire, and in so doing may have a better chance to tame 'the Beast'. The physics of Fire behaviour are taught as part of their training, but understanding 'the Beast' comes through experience.

Fire spirits are different from Earth spirits in that one cannot simply go out into the forest and hope to meet them. To do so could lead to disaster. However, a wild Fire spirit can be easily created/summoned by clearing an area and building a small Fire. Obviously, quite a lot of caution is necessary to contain the spirit...and the Fire itself. To let it get free of the space provided for it would be unconscionable carelessness, and could result in a lot of unnecessary destruction. Never forget Fire safety!

Once you have invited a Fire spirit and provided a controlled flame for it to manifest within, Fire spirits are uniquely cooperative. They can be enticed to reveal the future or the present in another location, or persuaded to assist in acts of magic. Remember that Fire represents action. For Fire spirits, the joy is in the 'doing'. Little thought goes into reasons or consequences. Again, caution is advised here as freeing the spirit to perform magical acts must not also free the flame itself.

Seeing the spirit may happen spontaneously, but can be done intentionally by unfocusing the eyes and looking at the space above or around the flame itself, where the heat seems to make the solid objects present to waver to human vision. The Fire spirit may test you with fear and cause you to look away, or you may have to blink to re-wet your eyes several times in the process of getting to know your Fire spirit.

If you wish to develop a relationship with a wild Fire spirit, you can do so by choosing a location where you can re-light a Fire again and again. Once you invite and make contact with a Fire spirit, you can call it again the next time you light the Fire in the same location. This is easiest to accomplish if you name the spirit on first meeting, or better yet, allow it to name itself.

If this method of repeated communication is chosen, I recommend making friends with the Earth spirits in the location first, and explaining your purpose to them before you begin, lest you frighten them with the conjuring of Fire spirits as well as open flame, with all of its destructive potential. A promise to keep the Fire and its spirit contained would not go amiss.

Leaving a gift for the resident Earth spirits after each session is always a good idea. As for the Fire spirit itself, the greatest gift you can leave is a promise to rekindle the Fire, to once again allow it to manifest into life. Flame spirits receive their gifts during manifestation, in the form of fuel. Other forms of wild Fire spirits besides flame spirits are most likely to be seen through spontaneous sightings.

The spirit of Fire works in conjunction with the human spirit in that the life force is fed by the very presence of a Fire spirit, which is why dance therapy is often a very successful form of treatment for certain medical conditions. The human spirit is naturally drawn to Fire, harmonizing in a symbiotic exchange of energy which is not unlike the melding of flame which occurs when two sources of flame meet and combine into a single, much larger Fire. Encounters with Fire spirits can be very invigorating, yet once again, there is potential for danger. There are some people who are unable to reconcile the feeling of communing with the spirit of Fire with the separate existence of their own life force, and these people may be at risk of losing control and being seduced by the allure of arson after a significant encounter, which can be addictive much as some people can easily become addicted to certain substances (alcohol, drugs, caffeine etc.) For these people, the intensity of the Fire spirit becomes their addiction. They crave more, and may act spontaneously and irresponsibly to fulfil the craving. The spirit of Fire should never be taken for granted.

I said in *Spirits of the Earth* that nature spirits will sometimes flit about and confuse human visitors. The Fire spirit has its own version of this intentional disorientation, and the danger with flame spirits in particular is that it may use a chaotic situation to try to break free of its containment. Fire spirits are not shy in the way of Earth spirits. They will happily burst forth into manifestation and dance wildly for all to see at the slightest provocation. The question is, did you really see a spirit dancing in the flames, or in the wake of the dance, or was it only a trick of the light?

To Seek Fire Spirits in the Home

Obviously, Fire should be avoided in the garden in general. However, outside lanterns, torches or even a barbecue are places where Fire can manifest in conjunction with the Earth and Air spirits of the garden. Any source of light is also an area of Fire spirit activity. I sometimes visit a friend who owns a farm, and who often places a circle of garden torches around the bonfire area whenever there is a social event occurring on the farm. The circle of Fire, combined with the central bonfire, creates a natural high energy 'buzz' which is very conducive to the party spirit. This is reflected in the success and popularity of these occasions.

Inside the home, there are many forms of Fire spirits which may be observed, particularly various forms of flame spirit. These include the spirits of candle flames and gas flames for some people as well as the traditional hearthfire for those who are lucky enough to have a hearth in this modern age. The hearthfire in particular is given to visions of attendant Fire spirits. The spirits of these sources of flame can be observed much the same as the bonfire spirit.

There are other forms of Fire spirit which can be found in the home. Dance spirits can of course be raised as easily indoors as outdoors, and perhaps more easily observed indoors. Again, sources of light reflect a spiritual essence in the light itself, and the spirits of these sources of light can be observed peripherally in the immediate glow around the source, although the strain on the eyes may not be worth it. Certain objects may be attended by a Fire spirit, for example, an incense burner spirit can become very much a part of the home and, much like the little black men and other elemental spirits, can be observed with peripheral vision.

Spirits of passion sometimes manifest visually, and can be very distracting during sex when one catches a glimpse of an unexpected movement in the room during the act. Of course, the home is a place where it is well to remember that the potential for manifestation of flame spirits is always present, and Fire safety which should always be observed anyway is particularly important in homes where Fire spirits may be called or invited into ritual. A home also contains a life force spirit which will come into being from the combined spiritual essence of the inhabitants. There are families who are aware that they have a 'family spirit', which is sometimes mistaken for a ghost, and a few of them have visual encounters of some description. The nature of this spirit, like Fire itself, is mutable and will change with the changing members of the household or the moods and experiences of long term residents.

Spontaneous Sightings

As I have said above, spontaneous sightings of Fire spirits do occur, but are less often recognized than with Earth spirits. A glimpse of a dance spirit. a passion spirit or even a flame spirit often happens too quickly for the observer to be entirely sure that anything was seen at all. If one were to stumble into the 'Land of Faerie' which would likely lead to encounters with a variety of elemental spirits, or to have some form of otherworld experience which involved Fire spirits, one might easily think that one had encountered one of the demons of Christian mythology or even stumbled into the proverbial Hell. Fire spirits can give a very powerful and aggressive impression. Such encounters do happen, but those few who experience this sort of Fire elemental 'close encounter' are even less likely to talk about it than if they had seen fairies dancing in the moonlight, which might also be a Fire spirit encounter.

There are exceptions of course, and there are rare occasions where a person might actually be driven to madness by the experience. In general though, spontaneous sightings of Fire spirits will be the elusive sort. Most of them are actually quite harmless, so long as nothing flammable gets out of control.

To See Invited Fire Spirits

Fire spirits which are invited into full ritual are the most likely to take visible form. The method to see them is still the same as with any flame spirit, although these spirits may be either flame spirits or guardians of some sort. A thought-form Fire spirit which is conjured into a contained space may even be partially seen without resorting to peripheral vision. It can appear as a distortion in visibility within the chosen space, but may take a more solid appearing form. However, this solidity could only be an illusion. Closer inspection would reveal constant movement in the substance of which the image of the spirit is made.

The spirits of Fire surround us much more than we usually realize. Visibility is always intangible with elemental spirits, yet certain circumstances are more conducive to our ability to see them than others. With Fire spirits, they are most likely to be seen during an act of magic.

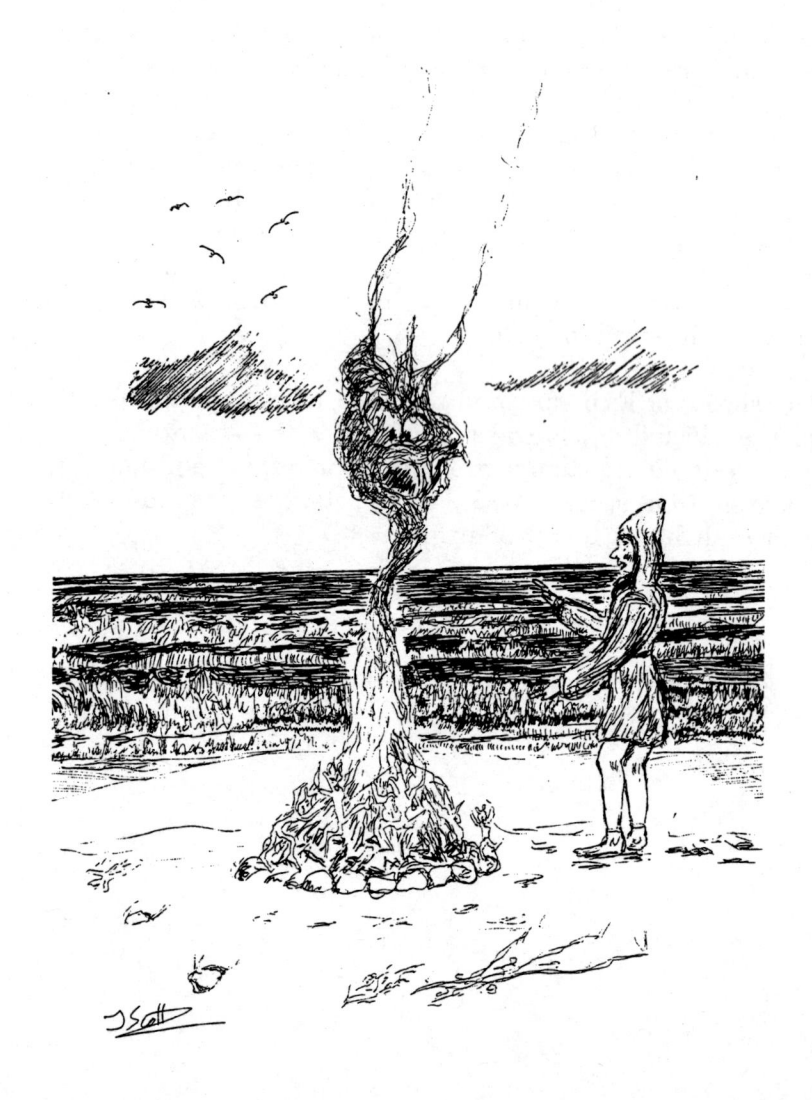

Chapter 6

Fire Spirits in Natural Magic

Fire spirits, much like Air spirits, are very spontaneous by nature. It follows that Fire magic is also prone to spontaneity, in several different ways. One might be suddenly driven to perform an act of magic, which by its very driving force could then be classified as Fire magic. A specific spell which involves the element of Fire might easily move into an unexpected direction, which could get rather dodgy if not downright dangerous, yet is an extremely powerful situation for the magician who is able to keep the progression balanced and under control. A Fire spell could directly cause something to happen spontaneously. In all cases, the relative stability of the result is likely to be dependent on the relationship between the magician and the Fire spirit involved.

Fire spells which do not specifically call upon the assistance of Fire spirits will attract them anyway, so it is just as well to become familiar with their nature and to invite their participation in one's Fire spells from the start. These spells may include divination, love spells, healing, protection, or purification. Fire spells are specific to action, change, Will, progression and passion. Magic itself is the process of change (in conformity with Will, as Aleister Crowley put it), so abstinence from the use of Fire spells and spirits in order to avoid the dangers is really a rather futile gesture. Fire spirits are naturally attracted to any spell which involves action or change. If a person wishes to practice magic in any form, one might as well embrace the power of Fire, thereby allowing oneself to determine the parameters within which the spirit of the Fire shall be contained.

Fire, for all its dangers, can be contained.

Indoor spells should obviously be directed toward a contained space such as a hearth or a candle flame. Outdoors, a safely prepared bonfire, campfire, or even barbecue is recommended if an actual flame is required or likely to occur. Attendant Fire spirits can be cultivated in specific places, especially a hearth or outdoor Fire pit.

Not all Fire spells require flame. Fire spells can be created through such things as ecstatic dance or even through the generation of strong emotions, but extreme caution is recommended with this practice. Strong magic of this kind can cross the line, as I learned the hard way many years ago when such a spell got out of control and burned down the house I was living in. There was no source of flame at fault and the Fire department never determined the cause of the Fire. The house simply spontaneously combusted. Always determine your parameters with Fire magic, unless you are prepared to deal with potential consequences.

Fire can be frightening, yet this too can be used in magic. As I said above, strong emotions; passion, anger, jealousy, can all be used very effectively in both spontaneous and ritualistic spells. Fear magic, although very unstable, is no less powerful in effects than anger or passion and can be a source of great control in situations where fear must be overcome. Firewalking, for example, is an act of magic which requires rising above one's natural fear of Fire in order to walk the hot coals. The sense of elation which accompanies this accomplishment is intensely magical and could easily be put to use in magic. Inviting Fire spirits to participate in the ritual from the beginning should come naturally to a magician who routinely works with elemental spirits.

Fear can also be put to magical use in crisis situations, where spontaneous magic is the only option. The magician who is experienced in the use of Fire magic and the nature of Fire spirits knows that s/he can rely on a very powerful force when need arises. Spontaneous Fire magic is very chaotic, but it is also very effective.

Fire has a long history in folklore and legend for its natural magical powers. Associations of Fire with spiritual light exist in nearly all civilizations, including the pagan Romans, in Christian and Jewish mysticism and in Tantric Hinduism, among many others. Determining where the line should be placed between natural and ritual magic is difficult where the element of Fire is concerned. Many 'natural' practices such as the most primal act of using drumming and rhythm in dance magic might also be used in more formal ritual, while something seemingly ritualistic such as candle magic might also be a medium used for a spontaneous act of natural magic. One area which is reasonably defined as 'natural' is simple folk magic.

Folk Magic

Fire has been the subject of superstition throughout history, and naturally has also been the medium used in many basic forms of folk magic. Fuming, burning or smouldering an image, herb or other flammable object is commonly done in acts of folk magic, as is the use of candles (as stated), bonfires or blazes. 'Natural' Fire magic is practised in such places as near the hearth, beside outdoor Fires, or in a candle flame which was until that moment being used only for light. Sometimes an act of folk magic required that an object should be prepared and burnt, and often includes the scattering of the ashes to set the magic free.

A paradox of human nature arises in the use of Fire spells. Fire, more than any other element, has historically inspired fear and awe. This very emotional response adds power to the spell, yet it is in understanding the element of Fire that we learn its parameters and lose much of the fear of our ancestors, thereby gaining more control of the element as well as the magic we create through it. Too much confidence can weaken the force of the magic, yet Fire, as I said at the beginning of this chapter, is spontaneous. The potential for the unexpected is always present, and should never be forgotten. A healthy dose of caution not only keeps some of the awe of Fire alive in our spells, it also keeps us alert to the very real chaotic nature of this potentially very destructive element.

A Hearth Spell

One old traditional form of knot magic is to contemplate your desire while knitting and singing your chant before the hearth fire on a nightly basis. This example has also been used in both *Spirits of the Earth* and *Spirits of the Air*, as those two elements are also involved in this spell. The spell can be done without the Fire, but the Fire can be the driving force behind the magic. The participant creates something material (Earth) while singing the intent unconsciously (Air), but in contemplating the element of Fire, the participant draws in the smouldering force which gives vitality to the spell. The Fire should be contemplated, not stared into, yet enough hypnotic repetition of the activity and the song or chant is required to fall into trance. This spell can be even more effective if the song is directed specifically toward the spirit within the hearthfire. It sounds all too simple, yet it is a very effective form of magic. Be careful what you wish for!

The object which is created from this spell holds much of the magic within it, and thought should be given to the purpose it will serve before beginning the spell. It does not have to be a knitted object, it can be simply a piece of string with knots tied into it. I suggest knitting because it takes some time to create even a small finished project. If an item of clothing is created, it can be worn or given to someone who the spell is meant to effect. This obviously brings in the question of ethics. Someone who has asked for a spell to be performed would probably be happy to receive the item.

Another possibility is to burn the item in the hearthfire by way of completion of the spell. This would release the magic to the Aether. Obviously, this spell could also be performed in any Fire which is lit on a nightly basis, or a short version could be performed in a single session, for example by tying knots in a relatively short bit of string and burning the finished product.

Bonfires are well known centres of group magical spells. A group variation of the above spell could be performed, using a long piece of cotton string. The spell is opened and the bonfire lit, then the participants dance or march in a circle around the Fire, chanting the intent. This chant should have been agreed in advance. The string is passed from one person to another (the easiest way is to pass it to the person behind) and each person ties a knot, concentrating on the purpose, before passing the string on to the next person. When everyone has tied a knot or it has passed through the circle a specific number of times (3 or 7 in small groups), the person who started the ritual stops the dance and commits the string to the Fire, then the spell is closed.

Bonfires have held magical connotations for hundreds of years. Certain trees are traditionally burnt in the bonfire at festivals. The nine woods of the Beltane Fire are ash, apple, birch, yew, hazel, rowan, willow, pine, and blackthorn. Oak should never be used as it is the King of the Woods. Nor alder (sacred to Bran) nor elder (sacred to Hella, goddess of the Underworld). The Yule log traditionally burnt at Midwinter was traditionally made of ash.

Reaching Into The Spirit of Fire

Inviting a Fire spirit into A spell is a bit different than working with other elemental spirits. The potentially destructive power of Fire is all too apparent to a sensitive magician, particularly when working directly with flame, and requires the ability to balance "on the edge" of chaotic energies. Whether the magician is working with a small candle flame or a roaring bonfire, the basic approach is much the same.

As in other elemental spells, one begins by gathering the items which are intended for use in the spell. These may be many or few, or actually none at all in the material realm. Usually, the ritual implement which represents Fire to you (sword, athame, wand) would be used as well as a source of flame. As stated above, anything from a candle to a bonfire is equally suitable, although the larger sources of flame seem to inspire more Fire energy from the magician, and are often more conducive to dancing round which may be included in the spell. A magician who is very experienced at working with Fire spirits may need no implements or actual flame in order to call upon this sort of spirit, as the potential for Fire exists at all times within our atmosphere. A magician can fuel a spiritual Fire from within, as well as provide the spark. However, one must be wary of backlash when working from within. There is good reason for working with the symbology of implements in magic.

As with all magic, it is important to insure that you will not be interrupted during the spell. This is essential when working with Fire spirits. One begins by calming or meditating as with other spells and contemplating the purpose of the spell, but in a Fire spell the calm is quickly followed by a stirring from within. To reach a spirit of Fire, you must stir the Fire within yourself. The purpose of the spell should provide the exact approach. Strong, intense and wild emotions must be called up; passion and anger are the strongest, but not hatred as it is a weak and uncontrolled emotion. Passion and anger also have the potential to run out of control, but it is the ability to stir these emotions and yet keep them intensely controlled which will determine the success of the operation.

Stirring these emotions is done through an internal psychodrama, a willing of the specific emotion to arise. A state of passion or anger can be roused through external stimuli such as sexual stimulation or pain infliction, but these cross over to ritual methods and will be dealt with later. An appropriate trance state may also be stimulated through dramatic, hypnotic methods such as drumming and dancing freeform around the source of flame, the altar or just the centre of the ritual space. This, as described in *Spirits of the Earth*, is a matter of reaching a conducive state of mind, which must then be projected to the spirit of the Fire.

Unlike the Earth spirit spell, the conducive state is no longer a calm one. It is intense, powerful, possibly even frenzied. This is the nature of a Fire spirit, and the internal spirit which must be projected into your invitation. Like the other elemental spells, the invitation is most effectively done verbally in chant or song. This is an element where chant often works better than song, as the beauty of music could potentially dilute the intensity which has been worked up during preparation (there are, of course, some exceptions to this). The intensity behind the chant must match that which has been worked up in order to properly project the Fire behind your words.

As in other elemental spells described in this series, it is good to have a few lines prepared to begin with which can be taken into spontaneous chant as the participant decides. Another possibility is to have a specific chant prepared, usually about four lines, which will simply be repeated over and over for the duration of the spell. These two possibilities can even be combined, to state the purpose, add bits to make the request more specific or add power, and then launch into a repeated chant to build up the energy level to bursting. One wants to access one's own animal nature in order to build intensity for this sort of spell. Fire spirits respond to the strength behind the words, more than to the words themselves. However, as in any spell, be very careful about the choice of words and the possible alternate meanings. Fire spirits, like Air spirits, are impersonal. A spell could take an alternate course with the same sudden fierceness that a raging forest fire can change direction, trapping victims impersonally in the course of events.

In the case of Fire spells, the opening lines should be specific to the purpose rather than using a standard opening for all Fire spells. An exception to this might be if the participant has attuned to a specific Fire spirit who is to be called up on each occasion. Some examples for beginning Fire spells will be included in the appendix.

Apart from delivering the spell verbally, you may wish to add other ingredients to the working. Personal items, such as strands of hair or bits of paper with sigils or bodily fluids (or both, in the case of a previously prepared sigil) might be 'given' to the Fire. A statement of intent might also be written before or during the spell and burned in the Fire, releasing the message. This might be accompanied by wording such as; "I give to the spirit of the Fire my statement of intent, which is (read statement). Let the magic be released, as the paper which I give to the Fire is consumed." The trouble with this is that you must manage to burn the entire bit of paper. Any left over bits are an indication that there are obstacles to the working of the spell. You could get your fingers burnt in the attempt, either literally, figuratively, or both.

Hopefully you will have thought out your intent and potential consequences before beginning any Fire spirit spell, even a spontaneous one. According to folklore, inappropriate love spells last for 7 years (the first 6 months are pure hell and the next 6 1/2 years not good either) and spells which are done in passion or anger can all too easily be regrettable when the emotions have calmed again.

Fire is an element which must necessarily be respected if one wishes to avoid the inherent dangers. It naturally follows that Fire spirits must be similarly respected. In the world of elemental spirits, Fire is as necessary to the balance of nature as Air, Water, and Earth, yet is all too often avoided by magic users because of its potentially destructive nature. Yet Fire must be a part of our daily lives if we are to keep warm, to cook food, and also to enjoy the stirrings of passion in all of its guises. We cannot escape the stronger emotions, we can only learn to contain and direct them as one contains a source of flame. Once we come to terms with Fire as a necessary element in the balance of all things, we can begin to feel comfortable with this volatile element in the workings of serious ritual.

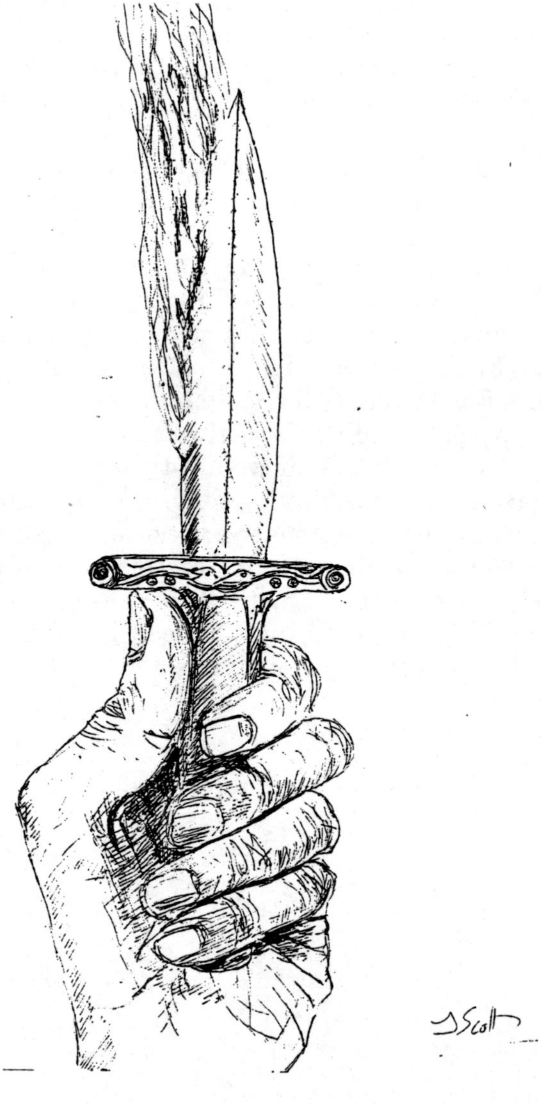

Chapter 7

Fire Spirits in Ritual

Rituals involving Fire go back throughout recorded history and probably long before. Fire has always inspired awe and respect among primitive peoples, and this reverence for an element which represents so much obvious power has only been partially diluted through modern science and understanding of the way that Fire behaves.

Cultural rituals involving Fire are numerous around the globe. In Britain, the tradition of hilltop bonfires still survives in some areas, although it no longer serves the purpose of a wartime warning system. Many traditions regarding Fire have survived their original Pagan associations through christianisation. For example, in the Isle of Man on Mayday eve, it was once traditional to burn all the gorse on the island in order to burn all witches and fairies who take refuge there after sunset (ouch!) Many of these traditions invoke Fire in its purification aspect as in the Christian sacrifice of lambs, which only now survives symbolically. The idea of this is that fire protects us from evil spirits, however these are defined in any given belief system.

Midsummer bonfires, Sun god worship in all of its forms, and the worship of Balder which comes from Norse origins are examples of Fire rituals and worship of Fire spirits. In the Isle of Man, bonfires are lit on hills and blazing wheels rolled from their tops in representation of the legend of how the island came by its coat of arms. The legend is that many centuries before the Christian era, the island was inhabited by fairies. A blue mist hung continually over the island which prevented mariners from seeing or even suspecting that an island was so near as their ships passed by. This continued until a few shipwrecked sailors were stranded on shore. As they prepared to build a Fire on the beach, they heard a fearful noise which issued from the dark cloud surrounding the island. When the first spark of Fire fell into their tinder box, the fog began to move up the side of the mountain, closely followed by a revolving object which resembled the three legs of men joined together at the upper thigh, spread so that they resembled the spokes of a wheel. The island was thereafter visible, at least part of the time. Some legends say that the mist is actually preserved by a perpetual Fire which is kept by the fairies themselves.

The word 'ritual' often calls up images of a formal altar complete with such accoutrements as a wand, sword or athame, chalice, pentacle as well as such practices as the formal calling of spiritual guardians or spirits for servitors or other purposes. Indeed, these trappings are commonly used in some form in many ritual traditions as well as by independent practitioners of The Arts Magical. The calling of spirits in some manner is well known in magic, but the calling of Fire spirits in particular is subject to dramatic images from various occultish 'B' movies and Dennis Wheatley novels. The more enlightened magician can make good use of these theatrical mental images when introducing the element of Fire into any ritual.

As I said in the previous chapter, the line between natural magic and formal ritual can be rather thin when dealing with the Fire element. Practices which apply to one often also apply to the other, and it is only through the formality of setting up an altar that the line is clearly crossed. It becomes a matter of the interpretation and intent of the magician, and in the end, the definition is unlikely to hold relevance to the magic itself.

Fire is unlike the other elements, in that a Fire spirit called up in ritual is more likely to be a natural spirit than a thought-form. This isn't to say that thought-form Fire spirits don't occur, quite the contrary, but that the element of Fire is usually available in an indoor ritual setting, either through a candle flame or other source, and with the actual element at hand in a setting which is as natural to it as any outdoor setting, it is actually much easier to invite a natural flame spirit into a ritual than to expend the energy to conjure the thought-form. The most common exception to this is the forming of Temple 'guardians' which are maintained on a permanent basis. Also, there are occasions when a thought-form might be appropriate for healing spells.

In a situation where a Fire guardian is conjured for the South of a circle (or East in the Hereditary tradition) it is a simple matter to use a natural spirit called from a candle flame, but for permanent guardians, it might be worth considering a thought-form as the natural spirit would have an inherent tendency to look for conditions whereby it might burst into flame at any time. A thought-form can be 'programmed' to express the essence of the Fire element without this need. This recommendation may seem contrary to my suggestion in the previous volumes of this series that quarter guardians remain consistent, i.e. either all natural spirits or all thought-forms, but the reader must decide whether it may be appropriate to make an exception for Fire if natural spirits are otherwise chosen for this purpose.

Calling Quarters

Obviously, if the reader practices in a tradition which comes with specific wordings for opening and closing rituals, it could be difficult to incorporate changes to accommodate contemporary methods for calling elemental spirits, unless the wording is already directed toward these spirits or the individual or group are open to making changes of their own choosing. This is an individual choice. However, even the strictest adherence to a pre-determined script does not preclude the ability of the practitioner to call the spirit of Fire non-verbally from within during the opening.

One of the most interesting openings for the Fire quarter which I have witnessed occurred several years ago at a large gathering in Sussex. The participants came from a variety of traditions, but had been individually recruited for this event ritual. Three people were chosen to represent each of the elements, and to dramatise the opening of their quarter according to the attributes of their specific element in very different ways. When it came time to open the quarter for Fire, the trio, skyclad and painted red, jumped out suddenly, seemingly from nowhere dancing like flames and shouting their incantation to the gods with all of the energy and flair that one should expect from the Fire element. It was very effective from a dramatic point of view. The ritual itself was in celebration of a holiday rather than a magical working for a specific purpose relating to Fire, but this sort of dramatisation might as easily have been applied to an intense magical working. The only problem would be the noise level, which isn't always convenient in more private rituals.

The magician who learns to stir this fiery spirit internally, without the necessity for elaborate dramatisation, can apply it to any ritual situation, no matter how controlled and sober the actual performance might be.

As with other elements, a Fire spirit can be invited into an object which is intended to represent Fire for one's rituals. Magical accoutrements which represent Fire might include a wand, athame or sword depending on individual choice, or a source of flame such as a candle or central Fire containment vessel of some description. A Fire ritual might be done with nothing but the Fire itself, or even through stirring up the spirit of Fire through a dance or, for the more experienced magician, simply through stirring up the appropriate emotional response to induce the spirit of Fire. A Fire spirit conjured in this way is no less real than a flame spirit, although an internally conjured spirit might well be a thought-form. This is, however, not always the case.

A representation for Fire can be kept in the appropriate quarter of a room used as a permanent Temple, or with caution in a room which is to be converted for ritual. Other decorations might be coloured red, perhaps mixed with other 'warm' colours like orange and yellow. Shapes which represent wavy, flame-like movement could be taken into account when choosing items to inhabit that quarter of the room.

The chosen item can be dedicated to the Fire spirit in a specific ritual for the purpose, or during the opening portion of a general ritual. As with the other elements, the wording of an opening may be pre-set in a format such as, "*Hail to the guardians of the South...*" etc., which can have a bit added to the end such as, "*...and we invite (name of spirit), spirit of the* (flame, athame, wand) *of Fire, to be guardian of the South* (or East) *in this and all our celebrations of the god and goddess, so shall it be.*"

As with other elemental spirits, Fire spirits respond well to spontaneity. However, I will include a sample 'Fire spirit dedication spell' in the appendix. Once a guardian spirit is established for the element of Fire and attached to an object to represent the element, it can be called again and again within the Temple or room which has been chosen, but can also be taken along for outdoor rituals.

Outdoor Fire Rituals

Choosing a location for an outdoor Fire ritual is similar to choosing any outdoor ritual location (as described in *Spirits of the Earth*), but must also include basic Fire safety consideration if a flame of any kind is to be used, as well as consideration for the local Earth spirits. A bonfire in a forest may look natty in a drawing, but in actual practice would make the various spirits of the forest (not to mention the wildlife) extremely nervous. A beach or open field is much more conducive to something like dancing round the bonfire. The most ideal outside location for a pure Fire ritual would be a hot place like a desert or volcano mouth, as the place spirits would include Fire spirits. Resident spirits of any place should always be considered in ritual. For a Fire ritual, it probably isn't appropriate to actually invite their active participation, only to ask their leave to perform the ritual in their world. Although I have explained that the potential for Fire spirits exists in all places at all times, these also are not ideal for inviting into your outdoor ritual, as the danger of residual energies manifesting after you have finished is rather too high. This is one situation where I recommend a 'bring your own' policy. The spell should be directed at the source of flame, whether it is a candle or only the fuel and match which lights the bonfire.

Fire Spirits For a Specific Task

A Fire ritual should always be for a specific task, as Fire is far too powerful an element for just playing around. Methods can vary widely, but will often include some form of ecstatic trance inducement. Animism in the form of masking or shapeshifting rituals are associated with Fire, as they directly access the life-giving principle. Dance and related breathing exercises, as well as hyperventilation methods (which are not to be toyed with without proper training) are commonly practised methods which remain keys to humankind's animistic nature and have been used for centuries in both primitive and civilized cultures. As civilized creatures, we still seek the magic of the primitive.

Fire has many underworld associations in mythology, and dramatizations of the appropriate myths are another path to inducement of the spirit of Fire within ourselves.

Apart from Temple guardians, purposes for evoking a Fire spirit are likely to involve some sort of definite action. Purification is one of the most basic purposes for Fire magic. Most of us know that Fire can sterilize an object such as a hypodermic needle or knife which must be used in otherwise non-sterile conditions. Similarly, the elemental associations of Fire are used in ritual purification. In agricultural communities of a more superstitious age, Fires are usually lit to the windward side of fields so that the smoke passes over the corn for purification. In ritual, a magician often begins by lighting a purification incense such as Dragon's Blood or Frankincense to purify the operation. In alchemy, Fire represents the purification of the soul. The only drawback to purifying oneself with Fire is that one cannot immerse oneself in the element without inflicting considerable damage to oneself...at least most of us can't and I wouldn't recommend trying!

It is through this purification aspect that Fire can be employed for healing spells. A Fire spirit sent into parts of the body which are inflicted with some diseases can potentially 'burn out' the infliction. Obviously, this practise has its own dangers and should only be resorted to in extreme circumstances.

Fire rituals are well known for negative purposes such as revenge spells, the trouble being that such a spell is very likely to reverberate on the sender. One would be better advised to burn out the hatred, or to use a Water spell to put it out instead.

Any spell which is intended to cause action or change of some kind could potentially employ Fire, but the reader is advised to consider other alternatives before resorting to this most powerful and potentially dangerous of elements. However, if circumstances are such that Fire is appropriate, then do it. Only set your parameters and proceed in confidence, not fear, as the spirits of Fire can sense the lack of control which accompanies fear and like a wild animal, will react accordingly.

As with all rituals, planning the procedure begins with gathering those things which will be used in the ritual. This, of course, requires at least a basic understanding of the appropriate correspondences.

Chapter 8

Fire Correspondences

Maybe the Earth is a Fire sign...?
--Wendy Lefay

Magical correspondences may be effectively meaningless to actual elemental spirits, but it is their meanings to us, as magicians, which serves a purpose in helping us to understand the symbiotic nature of elements in the natural world. No element works independently in nature, not even Spirit. Recognizing 'vibratory' relations between objects, human determined calendar events and celestial movements is entirely a human invention, yet systems of correspondences work in magic. If it is only our perceptions of them which make the association, so be it. So long as it brings a result, there is value in it. Of course, that is what Fire is all about; Results.

Fire correspondences must necessarily be those which deal with the life force itself, as well as those which deal with the actual element of Fire. Some of the more intense mysteries of the magical world, such as the associations of the Sephiroth of the Caballah to parts of the human body and the transmutation of elements in Alchemy, are appropriately designated to the element of Fire (correspondences for the alchemical elements and paths of the Caballah are already covered in *Spirits of the Earth*). Fire is represented by a

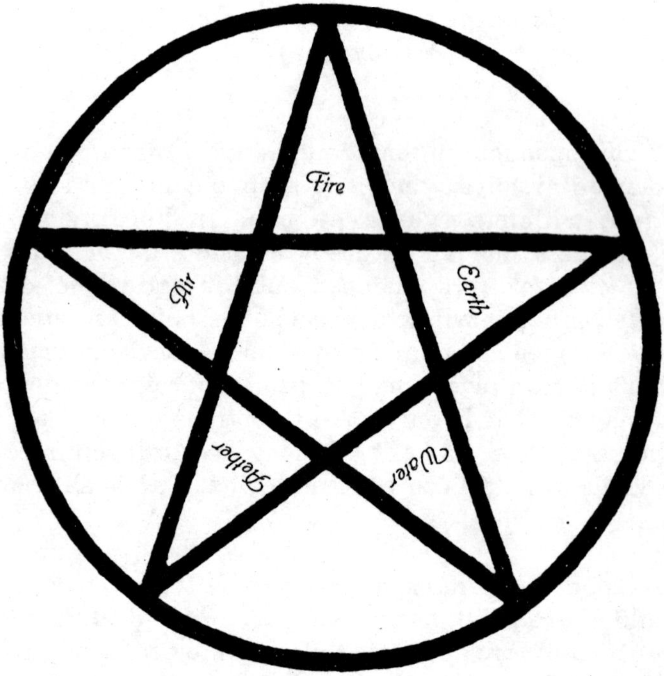
Fire
Air
Earth
Aether
Water

sword or athame (forged in Fire) in some systems, by the wand in others. Its colour is red, the season is Summer. The directional quarter is South, or East in the Hereditary system. Fire represents transmutation, passion, cleansing, and is associated with such things as lycanthropy and shapeshifting of all sorts. It is the reordering of the stuff of life which is represented in these mysteries. Fire is change, and change is chaotic by nature. The primordial, unformed chaos is always considered to be hot and molten. That which is in its molten state is ever changing, ever anticipating the reshaping of its components into an anticipated, but unknown, result.

It is interesting to note that in the beliefs of Red Indians, the soul, or spirit comes from the centre of the Earth, just as a baby comes from the centre of its mother. The Earth is our mother, the spirit returns to Her after death. The molten lava which seethes forth from an active volcano gives us imagery of the primordial chaos which lies unformed in the centre of the worlds we know, both physical and spiritual.

Fire is chaos, and chaos gives rise to order. It is only the form of the result which is unknown. Fire rules change, Will and passion as well as purification, fear, anger, jealousy and ecstatic trance. The signs of the zodiac ruled by Fire are Aries, Leo and Sagittarius.

The Tree of Life of the Caballah

Caballah, also spelled either with a 'K' or a 'Q', is an ancient Hebrew mystery. Like astrology, it is an in-depth subject which would require at least one whole book to explain in any detail, and indeed there are many books on the market which specifically cover the subject. Cabballistic correspondences have been listed in the correspondences section of *Spirits of the Earth*, but the most frequently referred to aspect of the subject is the system of Sephiroth called the Tree of Life.

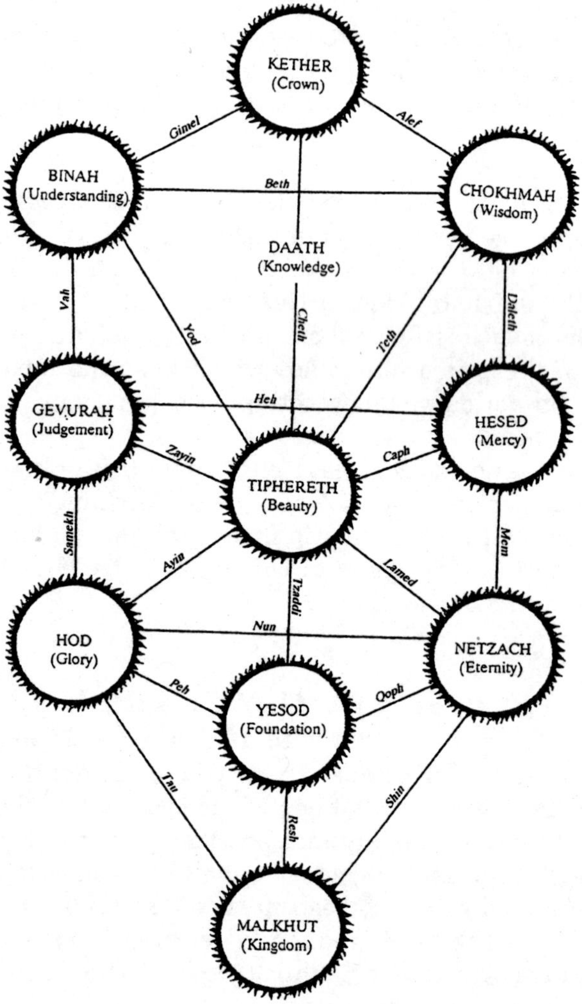
KETHER
(Crown)
BINAH
(Understanding)
CHOKHMAH
(Wisdom)
DAATH
(Knowledge)
GEVURAH
(Judgement)
HESED
(Mercy)
TIPHERETH
(Beauty)
HOD
(Glory)
NETZACH
(Eternity)
YESOD
(Foundation)
MALKHUT
(Kingdom)
Gimel
Alef
Beth
Vah
Yod
Cheth
Teth
Daleth
Heh
Zayin
Caph
Samekh
Mem
Ayin
Tzaddi
Lamed
Nun
Peh
Qoph
Tau
Resh
Shin

These are as follows;

1. Kether   (Crown)
2. Chokhmah   (Wisdom)
3. Binah   (Understanding)
4. Hesed   (Mercy)
5. Gevurah   (Judgement)
6. Tiphereth   (Beauty)
7. Netzach   (Eternity)
8. Hod   (Glory)
9. Yesod   (Foundation)
10. Malkhut   (Kingdom)
    Daath   (Knowledge)

These Sephiroth correspond (loosely in some cases) to parts of the body in a similar way to the Hindu Chakras, however, the two systems are separate and should not be mixed.

In Middle Pillar Meditation, the Sephiroth correspond to the centre of the body with those which are left and right creating an energy which manifests centrally. Following the diagram from the bottom and visualizing yourself in a sitting (cross-legged) position, Malkhut corresponds to the seat or base of the spine. Yesod, which represents emotions and feelings, corresponds to the naval area. The left and right correspondences are more approximate, with Hod and Netzach corresponding roughly to the loins, yet represents the solar plexus area. Tiphereth is the heart. Gevurah and Hesed are roughly the throat area. Also near the throat is Daath, yet this is representative of the unconsciousness and reflects Yesod in that if you turn the Tree upside down, Daath would then fill the place of Yesod. It represents the inner emotions while Yesod represents the more conscious emotions and feelings. Binah and Chokhmah are the brow area. Kether corresponds to the crown or top of the head.

Between the Sephiroth are the pathways of the Caballah which are marked on the diagram as well. As I said above, this is an in-depth subject which is beyond the scope of this book, but I make mention of it here in relation to magical symbolism.

The symbolism of the Tree of Life is only one example of tree associations with Fire. The Oak tree is considered sacred for several reasons, one of them being its tendency to draw lightning. Certain tree barks or woods have associations with magical intents when burnt. I listed the nine sacred woods for the Beltane Fire in an earlier chapter. Following are some tree associations for the making of incense.

Incense Correspondences

Protection;
Ash, bay, buckthorn, coconut, cypress, elder, gorse, hawthorn, hickory, holly, ivy, larch, mistletoe, mulberry, oak, palm, pepper tree, plum, pomegranate, quince, rose, rowan, sandalwood, wild service, wayfaring tree, witch-hazel.

Healing;
Ash, aspen, bramble, horse chestnut, elder, eucalyptus, lime.

Invocation;
Alder, bamboo, buckthorn, yew.

Purification;
Bay, birch, bramble, broom, cedar, gum arabic, lemon, osier, tamarisk, willow.

Fertility;
Banana, birch, coconut, fig, mistletoe, oak, olive, orange, palm, pine, pomegranate, quince, willow.

Divination;
Apple, ash, hazel, orange, poplar, rowan, witch-hazel. These can be used for making runes except orange and witch-hazel.

Love;
Apple, apricot, avocado, brazil, cherry, sweet chestnut, lemon, papaya, plum, prickly ash, rose, walnut, willow.

Prosperity;
Almond, horse chestnut, gorse.

Planetary Rulerships for Incense Making

Sun (self-integration);
Balsam, bay, benzoin, cashew, cedar, citron, frankincense, grapefruit, gum arabic (acacia), hickory, juniper, hemlock tree, lime, mistletoe, olibanum, orange, palm, pine spruce, thuja, walnut, witch-hazel.

Mercury (communication);
Almond, ash, cassia, hazel, mace, mulberry, pecan, pistachio, pomegranate, rowan.

Venus (unity, love, friendship);
Apple, apricot, avocado, banana, birch, bramble, cananga, cherry, damson, elder, guelder rose, hornbeam, magnolia, peach, pear, persimmon, plum, rose, rosewood, spindle, wayfaring tree, whitebeam, ylang-ylang.

Mars (action, war);
Dogwood, gorse, hawthorn, larch, pepper tree, prickly ash.

Moon (nature's rhythms, instinct, intuition, dreams);
Alder, aspen, bamboo, bergamot, broom, cassia, coconut, jasmine, lemon, linaloe, myrrh, olive, opoponax, osier, papaya, privet, sallow, sandalwood, willow.

Jupiter (expansion, learning, wisdom);
Banyan, blackthorn, bo tree, cajeput, sweet chestnut, horse chestnut, clove, fig, fir, lime, lindon, field maple, great maple, niaouli, nutmeg, oak, plane, ti tree.

Saturn (contraction, limitation, formation, obstacles);
Beech, buckthorn, elm, eucalyptus, holly, ivy, mimosa, poplar, quince, tamarind, tamarisk, wild service, yew.

Pluto (transmutation);
Box, cypress.

Neptune (refining);
Ash.

Uranus (deviation and invention);
Cedar.

While incense has been associated with Air for its scent and smoke, the actual burning of ingredients toward this end is an act of Fire magic, as in the burning of the sacred woods. According to Dion Fortune in *Sea Priestess*, incense for the Fires of Azrael which is to bring insight into past lives and induce visions can be made from 1 oz. sandalwood chips, 1 oz. crushed juniper berries, and 10 drops essential oil of cedarwood. Other associations are;

Cypress to allay grief and help heal invalids.
Mistletoe to ward off evil.
Pine for purification.
Rose petals for healing.
Bay leaves and rowan leaves and berries added to divination incenses.
Gum arabic for spirituality and purification.
Cedar wood for sweat lodges, purification, or to get rid of bad dreams.

Readers who are interested in this subject are encouraged to read *The Enchanted Forest: The Magical lore of Trees* by Yvonne Aburrow (Capall Bann, 1993) for more detailed tree associations.

Numerology

Numerology is an old science which is based on magical correspondences with numbers. The subject can be rather complicated, but the simplified version which is available in many modern magical books is sufficient to the purposes of this book. Numbers represent progression, and therefore numerology or any system which is based on a science of numbers must necessarily be ruled by Fire. Remember that before assuming that accountants are dull people!

As I have said in previous volumes of this series, correspondences are useful when constructing rituals. Numbers are one of the most useful components in ritual symbology, and may be used in many different ways. Understanding the properties of numbers is an important key to understanding the magic in nature. They are expressed in sound and colour as well as in quantities and calculations. The old systems of planetary hours (i.e. the timing of ritual by the hours after sunrise) have mostly fallen into disuse, but the basic associations of numbers are crucial to some forms of divination and ritual methods. Some people fear numbers by habit (from early maths lessons) just as they fear Fire as a potentially destructive element. Complicated systems of numbers can be confusing for those whose aptitudes lie elsewhere, and are better not used at all than got wrong. However, the following simple methods and associations should be intelligible to anyone with a basic primary school education.

To calculate your name number, add together the numeric value for each letter of your name from the following chart;

1	2	3	4	5	6	7	8	9
A	B	C	D	E	F	G	H	I
J	K	L	M	N	O	P	Q	R
S	T	U	V	W	X	Y	Z	

Add together the individual digits of the resulting number until you have a single digit result, or the numbers 11 or 22. This should be done for your entire name as you use it, and can change if you change some aspect of your name such as use of a middle name or an abbreviated form of your name. Different books on numerology will have some disagreement as to exact meanings, but the following general meanings are attributed by one source to personalities with these name numbers;

One - Fixity of purpose and drive toward achievement of goals. One track minded, self-assertive, sometimes even obstinate and aggressive. Independent, do not take orders well but can be original and inventive, potential leaders. Resent advice and are not likely to follow it. Can be domineering.

Two - Soft sweet nature, quiet, tactful, even-tempered. Love peace and harmony. Get their way by persuasion and diplomacy. Change minds easily, put things off. Can be deceptive.

Three - Bold expression, versatility and vivacious. Witty, charming, have sparkle and are likely to succeed in life. Tend to be talented in the arts. Succeed without really trying through sheer luck and taking things lightly. Spread efforts in too many directions.

Four - Efficient organizers, down to earth, steady and respectable. Like routine, detail and hard work. Can be stern and repressive. Moody. Hard won success.

Five - Bright clever and impatient. Attracted to the unusual and bizarre. Loves travel and change in surroundings. Takes risks and is adventurous. Avoids responsibility.

Six - Number of domesticity. Kind, balanced and has many friends and good home life. Loyal, idealistic and conscientious. Long term success through arts or teaching. Can be fussy and gossipy.

Seven - Number of scholar and philosopher. Natural recluse, possible mystic. Dignified, serious, intellectual, non-materialistic. Penetrating yet dreamy. Dislike being questioned or argued with.

Eight - Power, money, material success or failure. Strong and practical. Rebellious, hard struggles. Eight is a spiritual number despite these material associations. Its symbol is a lemniscate on its side.

Nine - Mental and spiritual achievement. Idealistic, visionary and romantic. Sympathetic and impulsive. Inspiring, strong-willed, falls in and out of love easily.

Eleven - The number of revelation, and for people who have a special message to give to the world. Subjective, live by their own inner light and vision. Powerful personalities, given to self-sacrifice for their ideals.

Twenty-Two - Number of the spiritual master. These people are either successful, admired and respected, or can turn to black magic or crime.

The birth number is also found through adding digits together, for example 28 October 1956 would be added thus: 2+8+1+0+1+9+5+6=32, 3+2=5. The destiny number is arrived at by adding the birth number to the name number, and interpreted through numerical symbolism as follows;

One - Individuality, self-reliance, possibly egotism.

Two - Relationship, attraction, emotion, sympathy or antipathy.

Three - Expansion, increase, intellect.

Four - Realization, possessions, position.

Five - Reason, logic, domestic travel.

Six - Cooperation, marriage, reciprocity, the arts.

Seven - Contracts, agreements, treaties, harmony or discord.

Eight - Reconstruction, death, the going out of a matter.

Nine - Strife, enterprise, division.

Eleven and Twenty-Two can be interpreted from the first list. The above list, the reader may notice, corresponds closely to the associations of the Houses of the Zodiac. It is through such common symbols that the workings of magic correlate with nature and the universe. This works in harmony with our own ability to access information through various forms of divination.

Chapter 9

Fire Thought-Forms

Constructing a Fire thought-form elemental is very much like the formation of any other thought-form, however, certain precautions are recommended to accommodate the potentially destructive nature of the element of Fire. More than with any other such elemental, the Fire thought-form must be contained within parameters to avoid possible disaster.

Having begun on that ominous note, let me assure the reader that with proper forethought, the Fire thought-form certainly is containable, far more than either an Air or Water thought-form, and like the roller coaster in an amusement park, can actually be far 'safer' and better controlled than some of the seemingly less dangerous rides.

Fire, as an element, is somewhat predictable compared to an element like Air, and can be specifically focused, as any demolition expert can tell you. Mastering the art of focusing the element creates an incredible level of power, and this is why it can sometimes be worth some risk of handling a volatile element to achieve an otherwise unachievable end. The risk is minimal if one knows the behaviour pattern of the element, and the proper safeguards.

Obviously, the choice to create a Fire thought-form is not to be made lightly. There are circumstances which warrant the unleashing of potentially destructive forces, but it is not an

92

element to play with just for the sake of feeling powerful or impressing one's friends. Handling Fire spirits of any form requires a degree of self-responsibility, even more so for thought-forms which are an extension of the will of the magician. An undisciplined magician would only be able to create a chaotic and ineffective thought-form, causing him or herself more trouble than it was ever worth. While chaotic methods might be used to stir up energy for the spirit, focusing the direction of the thought-form is an exercise in bringing order out of chaos as precisely as the demolition expert mentioned above can focus an explosion to completely destroy a single building within a concrete jungle without inflicting a single scratch on the neighbouring buildings.

Another advantage to Fire thought-forms besides pure, concentrated power, is that the natural life span of Fire spirits is shorter than for the other elements. A Fire begins and ends with the finish of its fuel supply. The clever magician can use this aspect of the natural order of things to create a spirit which expends a burst of energy toward a specific purpose, then dissipates harmlessly back to its source.

However, one must always remember that thought-form elementals can and will behave independently if given a chance, which brings us back to the subjects of focus and responsibility. Very specific purpose and direction must be established during the formation of the Fire thought-form. For example, a general spell for change in some aspect of your life would not be appropriate for a thought-form, yet a specific change may well be best served through this form of spirit. A spell to incite passion or to purify something could possibly be accomplished through a Fire thought-form, but care must be taken to avoid total consummation of the subject, whether it is on a spiritual or a material level. Fire thought-forms might be employed to add force to another spell, to employ the driving force of the element to any purpose. They can certainly be used to stir up a situation which has fallen into complacency, but this is certain to create some form of chaos which the magician must then be prepared to direct. For example, one might employ a Fire elemental to change a job situation which has stagnated, but the result could veer from an intended direction like job progression into a period of frequent job changes. Yet with Fire, this direction can be more easily predetermined with planning and specific wording in the spell.

Many people would be tempted to employ a Fire thought-form for a revenge spell or other destructive purposes. While there is potential for unqualified success with this method, there is also a strong potential for getting well out of hand. Success with this sort of intent could go farther than the magician intends or effect innocent bystanders. More dismaying to some people is the potential for rebound. Whatever the reader's personal views on magical returns may be, one must remember that a thought-form begins and ends within the magician's own energy source. Extremely negative energy sent out and then reabsorbed can be extremely harmful to the originator.

One area where a Fire thought-form can be very beneficial is in certain kinds of healing spells, specifically those which require destroying the source of disease. Again, this is not recommended for inexperienced magicians. The art of locating and eliminating disease within the material body is precise in magic, even as it is for a surgeon's knife. Overdoing it could possibly cause real harm, although there is an even chance than a magician operating beyond his or her skill level might be simply ineffective. A sample spell for healing in this way is included in the appendix.

An obvious purpose for creating a Fire thought-form is as a quarter guardian. As I said in a previous chapter, thought-forms are actually preferable for Fire guardians as they can be more easily contained, i.e. programmed to protect without destroying. Whatever purpose is required, the most important work is done during the creation of a thought-form elemental spirit.

Creating a Fire Thought-Form

Obviously, a formal ritual setting is most conducive to keeping containment intact for this operation. The purpose for the thought-form should be predetermined and very specific. No other business should be attempted during the ritual. Focus is essential both to success and to maintaining control.

Set up and open the ritual by your own chosen methods, or suggested methods from the appendix. Focus your intent on a place chosen for the formation of the spirit. This is already allowed for in the suggested ritual, but if you are using methods of your own, careful consideration should be given to this choice. A candle flame may be the easiest choice. It is best if things are set up in a way that allows you to walk around the chosen place. If working in a group, all participants should work together to keep their focus on the intent, and to keep this focus directed toward the chosen location for the spirit. A simple chant can help with this.

If, at any point of the ritual, any participant feels frightened, out of control, or just 'wrong' about the ritual, the operation should be aborted and the ritual space thoroughly banished. This is particularly important with Fire.

Circling the focal point and raising the life energy for the formation of the spirit works as with other thought-forms as described in *Spirits of the Earth* and *Spirits of the Air*. It is the concentration of the magician or group's energy which gives rise to this force.

Examples for wording can be found in the appendix, but there is more to the operation than repeating words. It is the art of focusing raw energy and spinning it in a spiral motion while circling which provides the required fuel for this Fire spirit.

Once the individual or group is satisfied that the Fire spirit is formed, it must be released to perform its task as described in the examples. With Fire, this release should always, ALWAYS include a subsequent destiny for the spirit, either to return to its source or to dissipate harmlessly. The spirit can actually be programmed in many cases to be fed by the need of the intent, which eliminates the source of fuel once the purpose is accomplished and the need no longer exists.

Note: Although most thought-forms are only slightly visible to physical sight if at all, Fire thought-forms can manifest more physically if enough energy has been put into their formation. This could be rather disconcerting to some people. If a decision is made to try to raise a Fire thought-form, all participants should be aware of the necessity for strictly containing the spirit from the outset, and should be of an emotional disposition to deal with the unexpected. One case of panic among a group could lose control of the entire situation. Be careful what you wish for!

After the release, close and banish, but be sure to banish against residual energies much like those described in Spirits of the Earth. This is important with all elements, but especially so with Air and Fire. Fire has much in common with Air regarding the behaviour of chaotic peripheral energy.

As I said above, some Fire elementals are fuelled by the need for their purpose, but this is only possible in short term spells. For a Fire to last any length of time, it must have a fuel source, so many spells will require that the thought-form is somehow sustained.

Sustaining a Fire Thought-Form

Fire thought-forms which are not specifically programmed to dissipate at the completion of their task can be carefully reabsorbed, or sustained for longer purposes. A quarter guardian would need sustenance, as would a spirit with a continuing purpose, perhaps in a protective capacity.

I have explained in the previous volumes of this series that these sorts of spirits are sustained through the energy of the magician, and care must be taken to insure that this doesn't become too much of a drain on oneself. Fire spirits probably require more energy than any of the other elements, however, there are fewer purposes which would merit this continuance of a Fire thought-form than with the other elements.

One must never allow a Fire thought-form to simply continue unregarded after completion of its task. Precautions should always be in place for dissipation or reabsorption unless there is a specific reason for the spirit to continue to exist. Then, sustenance for its continuation should also be prearranged so that it is not left to forage for its own energy source, like a spiritual wildfire.

The Fire thought-form is best fuelled through repeated rituals for the purpose (see appendix). I have suggested with other elements that repeated contact in regard to the purpose will serve the purpose, but more is needed for Fire. The force of Fire is such that the impassioned quickening of Spirit through ritual is required to some degree to sustain it.

For a quarter guardian, this could be accomplished during ordinary ritual openings by making a point of stirring up the appropriate energy during the part of the opening for that quarter. A bit of frenzy or focused emotion of a strong nature; passion or the driving force which is almost anger perhaps, can be introduced into most ritual methods.

For a protective spirit, short daily rituals focused on securing that protection are quite sufficient. Other long term purposes can also be sustained through regular rituals, daily, weekly, or perhaps less frequently as the need requires. The main idea is to effectively repeat at least a part of the original ritual to keep renewing the essence of the spirit.

One purpose which may require renewal of this sort is maintaining a Fire spirit for divination. Some forms of Fire spirit divination, such as Fire gazing, can involve the repeated calling of the same Fire spirit each time a divination with the same source is required. These can be either natural or thought-form spirits, depending on the skill of the magician and the sort of information required. In most cases of divination, a natural spirit is actually preferable, but there are exceptions. The traditions of divination with Fire are well established in the history of magic. The historic methods may seem few, but some have been added over time.

Chapter 10

Divination With Fire Spirits

Firegazing in some form is of course the most widely known form of divination with Fire. Whether or not the firegazer intentionally involves a Fire spirit is another matter. There are relatively few forms of divination which are directly associated with the element of Fire, however, a Fire spirit could be summoned to help in many forms which may have other elemental associations.

Firegazing itself, whether it is done with a candle flame, a hearthfire or other larger Fire, is essentially a method of scrying. One could just as easily gaze into the distortion caused by heat rising from a road or even turn to other elements and seek visions in a crystal ball, a patch of fog, or a pool of water. The only real difference is the medium within which one seeks the visions. It is the act of consulting the spirit of the flame which makes it a form of Fire spirit divination. This can be done by various methods, the first and most obvious being to directly petition the flame spirit for visions. Other methods of soliciting the assistance of a Fire spirit for divination would include ecstatic dance, formal ritual to a Fire spirit or even raising energy through strong emotions and directing them to the purpose, although this would require rather a lot of discipline.

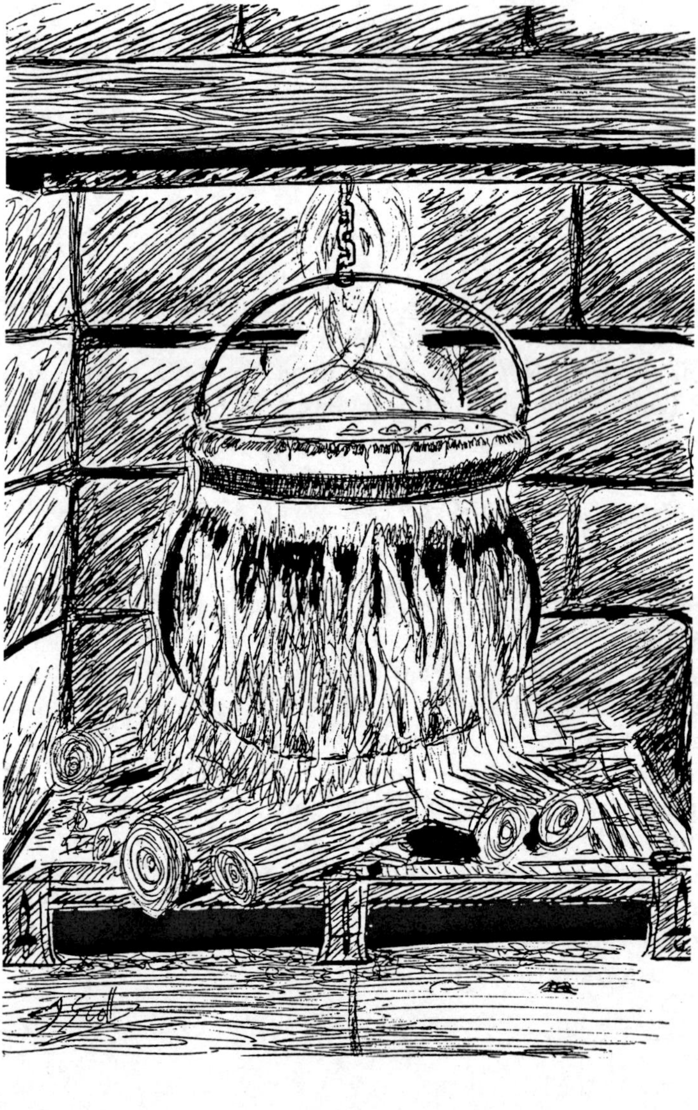

Many Fire rituals either for divination or some other purpose are accomplished by dancing around a Fire of some sort, raising the Fire spirit through the dance and focusing within the flame for the Fire spirit which will have been 'fed' through the raised energy as well as by the actual fuel for the Fire. For this sort of ritual to be used for divination, one person should be selected to seek the visions or to direct the intent. This method may be a bit over the top for most divinations, but can be very effective in times of crisis when the human mind is too preoccupied with worries to concentrate on more gentle methods. For ordinary purposes, a simple incantation to a hearthfire or campfire spirit is sufficient. Even a simple candle gazing, with some form of petition to the spirit of the flame, is often enough to answer daily questions. One thing to remember though, is to seek your visions in the space just above the flame rather than to stare into the candle flame.

In any method of Fire scrying, care must be taken not to damage the eyes. Fire gives light, and the eyes can be sensitive. A candle flame might be more damaging than the wider expanse of a raging bonfire. Sometimes unfocusing the eyes can help, as well as being conducive to trance states which are always helpful in any form of divination.

The benefits of mastering the art of Fire gazing are that once one learns to do it, it can generally be done as needed with any source of flame, and that it is an easy form to learn compared to many other forms of scrying. Crystal gazing for example, can take quite a lot of practice to master, but firegazing tends to draw the attention into a natural trance with little trouble. Fire spirits are outgoing by nature, and not inclined to keeping their secrets as are most divinatory spirits. If anything, they can be far too brutal with hard facts, which are often lacking in the protective symbolism which is usually a feature in other forms of divination.

Methods of divination which involve Fire, besides firegazing, do occur in folklore and tradition. There is an old tradition in Wales, wherein women congregate to learn their fortune from the candles they carry. Many forms of candle divinations occur in both old and new texts using such methods as setting up candles to represent a number of choices and recognizing the first to burn down and sputter out as your answer, or using the wax of a candle of an appropriate colour either to the element which represents the question or to some other colour association, to meditate on the question and then pour the melted wax into a glass or pottery vessel filled with cold water. Interpreting the shapes of the wax drips could be a bit tricky as it is far too easy to interpret any self-divination as one would wish it to be, but there are some basic guidelines: Spirals=reincarnation, or renewal. Circles=eternity and fertility or completion of a goal. Broken lines=scattered forces, lack of focus. Dots indicate that the question is too complex for an answer through this method, or that there is not enough concentration.

Invoking Guidance From Fire Spirits

Asking a Fire spirit to oversee or guide a divination by a chosen method which is not specifically related to Fire is fairly simple, but not often appropriate. The exception would be in a case where strong emotions are involved and likely to cloud the objectivity of the diviner. In this case, invoking or evoking a Fire spirit can actually absorb much of the negativity or excess energy being put into the divination.

Care should be taken not to overdo any conjurations of a Fire spirit which could manifest itself. Having one's Tarot cards burst into flame in mid-reading could be a bit off-putting at the very least! And no, I'm not just being facetious. Having got my fingers burnt (almost literally, it was just the house that burnt down actually) by a Fire spirit which spontaneously manifested in ritual in my younger days, I feel compelled to caution the reader against making similar mistakes. They can be good learning experiences, but Fire out of control has obvious dangers.

An incantation for this purpose should be specific and preferably directed toward a well contained source of flame. To evoke a Fire spirit's assistance in an indoor reading, a candle is the obvious choice, preferably a votive or other contained candle. The diviner prepares the runes, cards, or whatever for reading and as part of asking the question, directs his or her attention to the candle and invites the Fire spirit in a manner such as;

*"I call the spirit of this flame
to burn brightly with the force of my* (anger/ passion/ hatred),
*to clear my mind of all distraction
and to show me the way to the answer which I seek."*

The reader then asks the question aloud and proceeds with the reading, staying focused on seeking the answer to the problem at hand. This addition to an otherwise established divination method can clear away the rubbish of strong emotions where the reader is personally involved and upset by a situation, and can have the additional benefit of channelling enough negative energy through the purifying flame to leave him or herself exhausted and able to rest, perhaps to sleep when the situation may have made this difficult beforehand. Using this method outdoors is much the same, but a small Fire (campfire sized) can be used instead of the candle, and is actually more effective. The divination method can determine which is best, cards generally don't do well outdoors but runes or a crystal ball are heavy enough not to blow away or into the Fire itself.

A similar incantation can also open a firegazing divination, but firegazing can also be used in less dramatic situations simply as a choice of scrying medium. To seek guidance from a Fire spirit for ordinary information seeking, an incantation such as the following may be used;

*"I call the spirit of this flame
to burn brightly with the light of illumination,
to clear my mind of all distraction
and to show me the information which I seek."*

The reader will notice that this incantation is much like the previous one, but the focus is changed slightly (but significantly). Less formally, one may simply speak to the spirit of the flame and directly ask for information or guidance, seeking visions just above the flame or inspiration which occurs on the internal, spiritual level. The latter requires trust in one's own intuition and both require the belief in one's own ability to interpret impressions correctly.

Keeping a Fire Divination Spirit

A Fire spirit can be 'kept' specifically for divination purposes. This is done by keeping a receptacle of some sort which can be used indefinitely, not just the same candle or even a candle holder which can all too easily be put to another purpose.

To keep a Fire divination spirit, a small receptacle such as a brass bowl on a fireproof stand is ideal. With just a few readings, the Fire divination spirit becomes attuned to the object, just as Earth spirits attach themselves to objects, and can be recalled again and again, even named if desired. If you wish, the object can be dedicated to the purpose in formal ritual.

The small flame can be continually 'fed' during the divination with small, dry leaves (preferably of a divinatory herb or bits of appropriate tree bark). Various incenses can be used, especially for starting the divination when the scent will help reach the semi-trance state required for any divination. An actual small flame is required for this rather than just the smoke (unless one wishes to conjure the smoke spirit instead, see *Spirits of the Air*). The idea is to keep a miniature campfire going during the whole of the divination. Appropriate woods are listed for various purposes in the correspondences chapter of this book.

Always remember Fire safety with this method, on the mundane level as well as the spiritual. All of the spiritual precautions in the world wont stop your curtains from catching Fire if the flame is made too big or too close to possible Fire hazards!

I would also advise moderation on the idea of calling god forms associated with Fire, particularly with indoor rituals and divinations. Respect for the potential destruction of this element is always advised, but especially with historically established Fire gods which have more independence about them than even the most competent magician is likely to have much control over.

Whatever form of divination one chooses, the choice to involve a Fire spirit is one which should be made from a position of responsibility. As mentioned earlier, they can be the most forthcoming of elemental spirits, but they can also be callous, relentlessly honest with disturbing information to the point of cruelty, and difficult to disperse if the diviner becomes upset or frightened during the divination. Still, there are circumstances where a Fire spirit is the most effective choice. It is down to the judgement of the individual diviner to make that choice, but my advice would be to consider the other elemental options first.

With proper caution and consideration for consequences, Fire spirits can become a welcome and familiar element in the the daily life of any reasonably responsible magician.

Chapter 11

Living With Fire Spirits

Fire can be friend or foe, it is a two-edged sword. The death and renewal cycle mentioned in *Spirits of the Earth* takes on new dimensions with the Fire element, representing the cycle of destruction of the old to make room for the new. Like the Phoenix which is destroyed in the Fire only to be reborn, the purifying transmutation of Fire is a cycle of cleansing and new possibilities.

The Fire spirits who become the harbingers of destruction do so not out of malice, but because it is their nature. It is we who must seek new beginnings from this natural cleansing process. In nature, lightning strikes a tree or sap pops tiny sparks in dry conditions and creates a forest Fire. The forest is cleansed, and new shoots soon follow. The animals flee the raging Fire, but some do not escape. Yet more will always breed. Nature can be cruel in its impersonality.

Fire spirits need not be feared, only respected. Used wisely, it is a friendly element which brings warmth and light as well as immense power. Used wantonly, it can turn suddenly into the force of destruction. Becoming aware of the nature of Fire spirits can give us the ability to contain our dealings with them within reasonable parameters. To ignore or abandon them out of fear would mean cheating ourselves of an integral part of the natural balance of the elemental world.

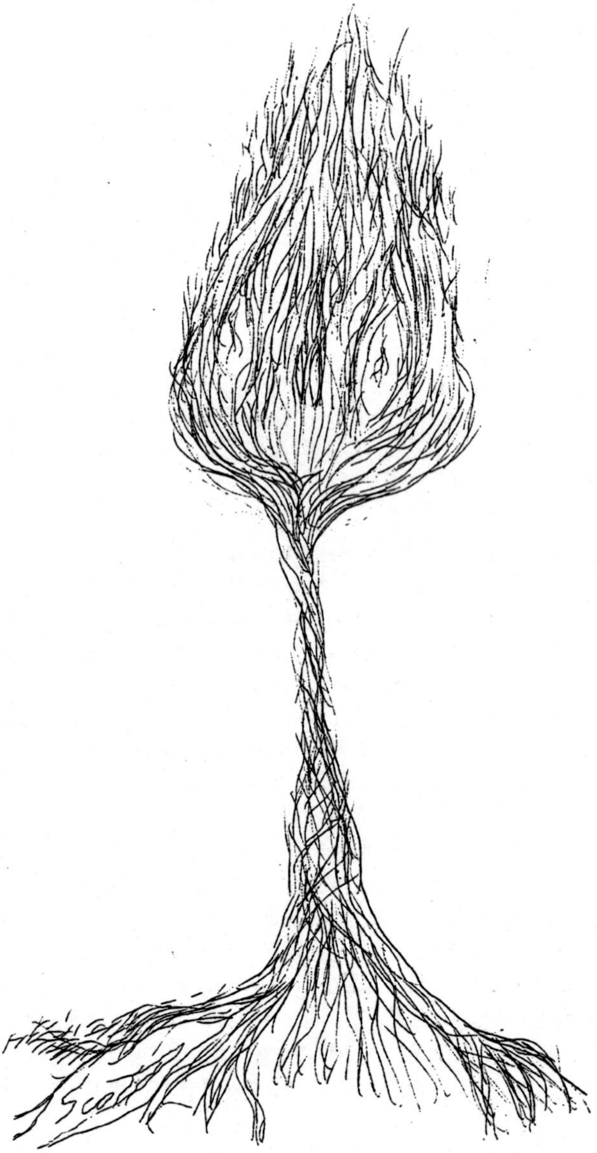

Without the drives and passions of Fire, we would only stagnate in mediocrity. The ecstasy of Gnosis and the power to send forth one's Will are very much mechanisms the life force and therefore of Fire, and are also a definition of magic.

The Divine Light, in whatever form, is much of what separates humans from the other animals. It is this aspect of our nature which all too easily gets out of control, turning our need to progress toward rampant technology which threatens to become our own source of self-destruction. Perhaps with more respect for the spirit of Fire within ourselves, it would be possible to learn reasonable parameters for this pernicious force.

Fire is also the driving force, the hunger, which leads us to Spirit. In nature, all things balance. It is in this need for balance that Fire spirits take their place, giving us aspects of the world which are essential to life as well as to the cycle of death and rebirth. In the balanced world of Spirit, there must be a place of warmth held for the spirits of the Fire.

> *"I, Fire, the Acceptor of sacrifices,*
> *ravishing away from them their darkness,*
> *give the Light."*
> --St. Catherine of Siena

Appendix

The following spells are intended as examples which can be used as models, or adapted as the reader sees fit. As I have explained in the previous volumes of this series, spontaneity and individuality are important factors in spell construction, particularly when working with elementals of any kind.

Fire spirits require a strong sense of purpose behind any spell which is going to be effective. Emotional content should be strong and personal. This is not easily accomplished by reading from a script for a basic spell. The reader is encouraged to add individual touches to any sample spell which is used, or better yet, to create one of one's own which is specific to the need on each occasion, referring to the examples only as a general guide to format.

Many readers will already have their own style of spell making, and may see the samples as only a reference for another person's construction style. We all learn from each other. For beginners, I hope the sample formats will be helpful. The important thing to remember is to always put the force of your own fiery spirit behind the magic you do when you want to attract the assistance of the spirits of the Fire.

An Opening For a Fire Spirit Ritual

As in all ritual openings, one begins by setting up the Altar. Even as this process is accomplished, the mind of the magician should be focused on the purpose for the ritual. This is especially true if one intends to open a ritual which is directed at the Fire element or if the intent is to summon Fire spirits of any sort.

The magical implement which represents Fire to you should certainly be included. For my own purposes, a specific Fire ritual would require the use of a magical sword. Even an athame on its own is not sufficient in my own opinion, as the athame is likely to also be used generally in other rituals. The sword, for me, is used in certain sorts of ritual and represents the epitome of Fire. Others may disagree. Other Fire symbolism may also be included, perhaps red candles, other red or orange objects, a central source of flame, or whatever else the magician feels is appropriate.

Alternatively, the magician may choose to work solely with internal energies, performing the ritual through dance or focusing the appropriate emotions. In all cases, focus should be on a central space rather than actually within the magician, which has obvious dangers.

The magician must direct the 'fiery' emotions into the ritual opening, regardless of its purpose. A Fire ritual which is intended for completely positive purposes must still invoke the chaotic energies which are associated with such ill-associated emotions as anger or passion in order to stir the forces which are required.

In most Fire rituals, I would recommend using original verse, but those who wish to begin with a standard opening might use something like;

"I invite the spirits of the Fire to join my ritual, and to give vigour to the progression of the magic which I do here now, even as the Fire gives drive and purpose to the progression of life and all that exists."

or,

"*I call upon the element of Fire for this ritual for* (change/progression/revenge/etc.) *and seek within the spirit of Fire for the strength and drive to accomplish my purpose.*"

Calling a Fire Quarter Guardian

As with the other elements, calling a quarter for Fire is often done according to established scripts, but can also be done spontaneously. With Fire, the important ingredient in the calling is to 'feel the Fire'. One may call the quarter guardian by a name or simply as the spirit of the Fire, which in the Wiccan rituals are referred to as Salamanders. A very basic calling which is consistent with those I have included in the previous volumes of this series is as follows;

"*I call upon the spirits of the Fire, of Will, of change and transformation, of drive and of the spark of life itself, to witness* (my/our) *rites and to lend the qualities of determination and fortitude to* (my/our) *magic. Let it be so.*" (or "*so mote it be.*")

A Sample Ritual Closing

As I have said before, the closing of a ritual should be consistent with the opening in most cases. Again, many readers will already have their own established practices, based either on a tradition or on their own developed practices.

The important thing is that there is a closing, and that the residual energies are thoroughly banished, parti-cularly in Fire rituals. The elemental spirits must also be thanked for their participation, in the closing of the ritual as well as when the magic brings a result. Example closings are as follows;

"*I thank the spirits of the Fire for joining* (my/our) *ritual, and for providing the spark of determination to my purpose.*

Depart now in peace to your natural realms, until next we come together in love and magic."

or;

"(I/we) *now release the spirit* (name optional) *of the element of Fire, and thank you for your assistance in this ritual for* (change/progression/revenge/etc.) *Let the purpose be accomplished, and the spirit of the Fire be released from this service and at peace."*

or;

"(I/we) *thank the spirits of the Fire, of Will, of change and transformation, of drive and of the spark of life itself, for witnessing* (my/our) *rites and for lending the qualities of determination and fortitude to* (my/our) *magic. Let them now return to their realms, until next* (I/we) *call upon them for their assistance. Let it be so."* (or *"so mote it be."*)

The Middle Bit

For some magicians, the 'middle bit' comes between the openings and closings, while for others, it encompasses the entire ritual. This is a matter for individual choice. When working with the element of Fire or with Fire spirits, I feel I must emphasize the need to banish the space at the end of the ritual. Some magicians actually banish both before and after a ritual, which I do recommend, particularly when working with Fire. Banishing might be considered an alternative form of opening. It's purpose at the beginning of a ritual is to clear the space completely of loose energies or spiritual entities, which prevents them from being effected by the magic which is then performed and possibly carrying some influence of it along with them later, after the final banishing.

One could visualize the process much like making a campfire. First, loose dry leaves and other bits which might blow away and start an uncontrolled Fire are cleared. Then the campfire is prepared and brought to life, after which it is extinguished and any loose embers stamped out in order to eliminate any possibility of them getting loose and creating havoc.

Magic reflects nature and natural laws. A campfire is made by humans, so is a magical ritual. Both require precautions if they are to remain under our control. One of the most basic rituals that one may perform with Fire, is simply to invite the spirit of the Fire (which already exists when the flame is kindled) into a flame, by way of recognition.

A Spell For Inviting Fire Spirits Into The Flame

This is a fairly basic procedure which can be done as a prelude to any Fire ritual. Open the ritual according to your choice of methods and kindle a flame, by lighting a candle or other controlled source of flame. For most Fire rituals, the intent at this stage is to connect with the spirit of the Fire in mutual recognition before going on to specify the purpose of the ritual itself. This can be a rather intense experience. The magic user who is fearful in any way should not attempt a Fire ritual, but should rather find another element, or the balance of all elements in which to perform the required magic. Also, losing one's nerve during the ritual should be dealt with by immediate and firm closing and banishing.

There is no real danger in communicating with the Fire spirit, however, it does cause an emotional reaction which can cause irrational panic, and a magician out of control can do harm to himself and others. To make the first contact, sit or stand in front of the source of flame, and project your own spirit and consciousness into the heart of the flame, taking care not to stare too intently with the eyes (which could be damaged by too much concentrated light). The invitation itself can come directly from the heart, or may go something like this;

"I invite the spirit of the Fire, to come to this flame and share my purpose, to inflame my spirit with the vehemence and passion of Fire. Let our two spirits be as one, your strength be mine, my purpose be yours, Let it be so." (or *"so mote it be."*)

If the invitation is to be for creating a Temple spirit or other home guardian, a slightly milder approach is recommended. A specific Fire ritual for home protection is NOT recommended, unless the home has been habitually vandalized or attacked in some way and some form of response to such a situation is required. This sort of plight requires an individual approach by a very experienced magician.

A general home blessing or Temple blessing ritual, which would incorporate all four of the basic elements, still requires some contact with the Fire spirit, but can be done on an emotional level as the actual blessing is spoken. The ritual could be done centrally on an Altar, or by addressing a representation (a red candle will do) in the appropriate quarter, which would be South or East for Fire. The Fire portion of the blessing for a Temple may go something like;

"I call upon the spirits of the element of Fire, and invite them to lend their qualities of drive and passion to this Temple and to the magic which will be done within it, to become a protective part of this place, and of those who practice within it. Let fortitude and Will prevail in all workings done here."

or, facing the appropriate direction;

"I call upon the Fire spirits of the (South/East) *and invite them to lend their passion and fortitude to this Temple and the Magic which will be done within it, to become a protective part*

of this place, and of those who practice within it. Let fortitude and Will prevail in all workings done here. Let it be so." (or "*so mote it be.*")

A slight variation could be done as part of a home blessing, as described in *Spirits of the Air*, by using either of the above but leaving out the bits about working magic. Note that the qualities of change and transmutation are not mentioned in these examples. This is because an emphasis on those qualities of Fire could have a destabilizing effect on a Temple or home, which is not advised. For outdoor magic, blessing a place by Fire is generally not recommended but rather a portable object which represents Fire can be brought along for the purpose, and returned to safely controlled conditions afterwards.

Inviting a Fire Spirit Into an Object to Represent Fire

I have pointed out that some people regard the sword or athame as the ritual implement which represents Fire, while others choose the wand. Either the wand or the athame is easily portable, while a sword is likely to be large and unwieldy for travel to anywhere where one might choose to perform a ritual, not to mention a bit difficult to explain to anyone who might happen upon an outdoor ritual. On the other hand, as a permanent Temple object, the sword is certainly more impressive for creating the 'otherworldly' atmosphere desired in a Temple, and is better suited to drawing protective circles on the floor if that is part of one's ritual practices.

The actual choice of object must fall to the individual. I generally recommend bringing the object into ritual just as an ornament for some time before dedicating it to active ritual use, as this attunes the object itself to the user or group. If decorations are to be added as part of the dedication ritual, the main part of the object and possibly the materials which will be used can still be present in prior rituals. As with objects which represent other elements, dedication of an object to represent Fire should be done as a separate ritual. No other business should be done during the same ritual. The only exception to this is if objects for all of the elements are being consecrated at once. Choose a time and place where you will not be interrupted. It can be indoors or outdoors, so long as there is a source of flame available. A permanent Temple object should be consecrated within the Temple.

Open the ritual according to your chosen method. If the object is complete, you can then launch directly into an invitation to the Fire spirit. If possible, pass the object through the flame as you issue the invitation, which may be as follows;

"*I call upon the element of Fire, to bring forth a spirit to inhabit this* (sword/athame/wand). *Let this spirit come willingly and without reservation, to become a part of the magic of this* (sword/athame/wand), *and to dedicate its existence to the purpose for which it is intended.*"

You may wish to specify a purpose at this point, or a generalization such as, "*to bring the magic of the element of Fire to my Altar.*" Close and banish.

You may wish to decorate the object during the ritual. If it doesn't take very long, it is best done during the stating of its purpose, which can be repeated in a chant if necessary to allow sufficient time.

To Sustain a Fire Entity

I have said before that sustaining an entity which has been dedicated to a specific purpose is primarily done through repeated use of the object, or through recharging it through repeated rituals. In the case of a ritual object to represent

Fire, this is very easily done. Fire spirits are more steadfast than the flighty Air spirits, and are always at the ready to burst out in full power. If the magic user has chosen an athame or wand to represent Fire among the ritual equipment, this object is likely to be present at all rituals and put to use in some way. For rituals which justify an emphasis toward the qualities of Fire, the object may merit special attention, perhaps an invokation to the Fire spirit within the object as it is passed through a candle flame. No further efforts are usually required to sustain a natural Fire spirit, but if a long period of time passes between rituals, a rededication ritual following the same or a similar format to the original consecration may be in order, and would certainly do no harm.

Simple Folk Spells and Other Magic

Folk spells which involve some form of Fire symbolism are primarily either purification or fertility spells, although any spell which involves the lighting of a candle can also be considered a Fire spell, possibly also incorporating other elements. Apart from the aforementioned examples of purifying spells, any spell which involves cleansing by Fire has its roots in folk magic, as do most fertility spells. The simple act of crawling through a holed stone is symbolic of the sex act, and an ancient form of fertility folk magic, as is jumping over a Fire.

The other most used form of folk magic which involves Fire is the precursor to modern sigil magic, the act of burning something which symbolises a desire, so that the wish is sent into the Aether. Many common spells involve Fire in some form, usually in conjunction with other elements.

A Basic Sigil Spell
Any representation will work as well in this sort of magic, but one of the most basic forms is to draw a symbol or write a sentence (be specific!) to represent a wish or need. Parchment paper is nice, but any bit of notepaper will do. Charge the sigil with some form of ritual. This can be a repeated chant, a full formal ritual, a sex magic charge, or any chosen form so long as the magic user achieves the state of 'vacuity', that feeling which one gets when working effective magic. Burn the sigil in the flame of a candle. Keep in mind that you will eventually have to let go of the paper as the last corner burns, so have some place, even a simple ashtray, handy for this purpose.

To Charge an Object by Fire
There are many ways to magically 'charge' an object, this is only one. It may be done as part of a longer ritual, or as a separate ritual between an opening and closing.

Pass the item through a flame either of a candle or of a larger source. Project yourself into the flame, feel the spirit within and address it as follows;

"*I call the spirit of the Fire to purify this* (object) *and to imbue it with the vitality of the force of life and magic, that it may conduct this force at my Will and pleasure.*"

The chosen phrasing can vary in accordance with the exact intent.

Cleansing by Fire
The possibilities of how an item may be cleaned by Fire vary according to their nature and flammability. Most ritual implements can be passed through a candle flame or other small flame. Those things which are not suitable for passing

through flame can be held above a flame, within a reasonable distance of the heat according to the material involved. Very flammable items can often be used to circle a candle flame, keeping far enough away from the heat to avoid damage while still encompassing the spirit of the flame. A basic chant is all that is needed for this, such as;

"I pass this (object) *within* (or around) *the Fire of purification, and ask the spirit of this flame to cleanse the essence of this* (object) *that it may be free of all defilement. Let this* (object) *be now clean and pure. Let it be so."*

A Fertility Spell

Fertility spells are numerous in folklore. Many could be found through researching books on superstitions, but I will include a simple ritual here which is based on seeking the assistance of a Fire spirit. It is best to perform such a ritual at a woman's fertile cycle if this can be determined, as any magic works best with a high probability factor. For women or couples who have medical problems which interfere with fertility, medical treatment should be obtained in conjunction with a ritual 'push' for the same reason.

This ritual can be done by a couple together, or by a woman alone who wishes to conceive and will be attempting to do so within a day of the ritual (whether it is with a partner or through artificial insemination).

Open the ritual according to your chosen method, or using a version of the Fire ritual opening included in this section. The ritual set-up should include a source of flame. A candle (red) will do, but a larger Fire would be good if possible. A camping holiday together in an isolated place would allow for a good campfire. Drumming music would be beneficial as well, even if it is recorded music.

Next, address the Fire spirit directly, invoking the spirit of passion within the element of Fire. This is best accomplished with body movements, dance if possible, and a repeated chant addressed to the flame such as;

*"(I/we) call the spirit of Fire, the source
of passion, of Will, and universal life-force
Let quicken the womb, a child conceive
The seed (I/we) now sow, in love the fruition (I/we) receive.*

Any verses you prefer are just as good, so long as the message is clear. The idea is to address the life-force aspect of Fire more so than the passionate aspect, otherwise the results could be a particularly passionate love-making session which fails to fulfil the actual intended purpose.

Repeat the chant while circling the source of flame, building to a sense of frenzy, but not exhaustion. If a couple are working together, choose a moment which feels right to sexually consummate the ritual. If a woman is working alone, build to that point but then stop and address the Fire directly, repeating the chant one more time, leaving a void to be fulfiled. Do not indulge in any form of release until such time as conception is to be attempted.

Close the ritual, but do not banish. It is very important in constructing this ritual that any wording specifies the appropriate aspect of the Fire element, and cannot be reinterpreted to indicate the calling of flame. This ritual is an exception to the 'always banish' rule. It requires being left with an expectant feeling, one of unfinished business.

One thing to note about any Fire ritual is that incorporating some action with which to stir the emotions is very conducive to attracting the interest of Fire spirits, as well as creating the appropriate mind set for this approach to the magic. The most obvious ways of accomplishing this are to use such things as dance, drumming, music which stirs the emotions and/or Altar decorations which form a visual association to Fire. Certain incenses can also bring the effects required, but this is better determined through trial and error than by depending on the names put on a range of incenses. What is effective for one person may not be for another.

Two of the more advanced methods of charging a ritual or an item are with sex magic or through pain, but these methods should be studied thoroughly before experimenting. There are books on the market specifically about sex magic (see authors Frater U.D. and Donald Michael Kraig), sometimes included in books about Tantra.

Pain stimulation has obvious scope for getting well out of order, but a basic method for trance inducement is to use a scourge lightly and repeatedly (just enough to sting a bit) on the area just above the cleft of the buttocks. Obviously this is easiest with a very trusted partner. It can be combined with chanting, rocking move-ments or other ritual methods. Obviously these methods would only be appropriate in very serious ritual.

Once the magic user becomes familiar with the 'feeling' of Fire, choosing appropriate sensory stimulation will come naturally. More importantly, s/he will be able to mentally call up that 'feeling' for spontaneous acts of magic, perhaps even for small matters such as striking the last match in hopes of lighting a campfire or invoking heat within a saucepan of Water which is taking too long to come to the boil.

A Few Sample Openings For 'Spontaneous' Fire Rituals

Spontaneous acts of magic such as I've just mentioned do not require a formal ritual opening and closing. They are some-thing which a magician simply does when required as naturally as most people open a door to get through it. However, there may be occasions where a spontaneous ritual is needed in order to deal with circumstances as they happen.

Obviously, a Fire ritual is unlikely to be the most appropriate choice unless specific circumstances, especially a crisis situation, demand that level of magic. In *Spirits of the Air*, I emphasized spontaneity. While spontaneity is important in all magic, in Fire magic, there is also a need for control. A short, spontaneous ritual opening can set parameters on spontaneous Fire magic, which helps to maintain that control.

It would not be possible in one book to anticipate every situation which could arise which might possibly require an act of spontaneous magic. First of all, the magic user must have experienced a Fire ritual in order to know what it feels like. It is the act of recalling that 'feeling' of Fire which will make an act of magic without the Altar or implements present possible. A very effective method for spontaneous opening is to chant in a drumming rhythm. An excellent illustration of this was depicted in the 1993 film, *The Secret Garden*. Three children, basing their actions on Indian mysticism which one of the children was exposed to in her early life, circle a Fire while carrying torches and chanting their desire, that another of the children's father should return home. The significance, besides the use of Fire, is the rhythm of the chant.

Sometimes even a small Fire is not possible to obtain in a situation of crisis. This is where the practitioner of magic must rely on experience. Visualization of a steady flame can be useful, but rhythmic motion of the body in time with a drumming chant, perhaps even performed silently with the internal voice, can stir the life-force aspect of Fire in a survival situation. The words should be specific to the situation, which is where the spontaneous aspect comes in. For example, a person trying to escape a burning building may chant petitions to the Fire spirits to clear a way that they may pass unharmed. In such a situation, it would be important to also invoke the life-force within to give oneself courage to take the path offered, as it is more likely to be a flicker than a gaping tunnel of safety. In a less dire situation, a person who is getting too cold while waiting for a bus may invoke internal warmth or a stalled car might be assisted to restart with similar petition spells. These rituals can be opened with a simple rhyme or chant to attract the notice of the appropriate Fire spirits. Judgement and quick thinking are important factors in spontaneous magic of any kind.

By the same internal mechanisms, a meditative contemplation of a visualized flame alone can be used to clear the mind of confusion or bring much needed enlightenment. Sometimes an opening can also serve as the body of a short ritual. Either way, the spirits of the Fire must be thanked and a banishing performed once the crisis has passed or the need for 'ritual mode' is otherwise finished.

Spawning a Fire Thought-Form Elemental

In the previous volumes of this series, I have recommended that creating a thought-form spirit should usually be done indoors. As in many things, Fire is the exception. The process could be done indoors, but is best done with a fair sized source of flame to centre the ritual around. This would be easier with some form of outdoor Fire pit.

The first thing to do is to decide why you wish to form a Fire thought-form. Perhaps a different sort of elemental would be preferable to your purpose. There are appropriate reasons for creating these spirits, but all other possibilities should be considered before proceeding. Thought-forms can and will get out of control given an opportunity. Fire thought-forms require very tight controls. They should always be programmed to return to the source of flame at the completion of a specific task. Even Temple guardians should be bound to a specific fireproof item which is kept permanently in the Temple.

Having made the decision, the method is very similar to other thought-forms. As mentioned, the focal point should be a source of Fire, although that could be encased in a metal triangle for the purist. Set up and open the ritual according to your chosen methods, then circle the Fire (deosil) while stating your purpose directly;

"*I wish to create a servitor, for the purpose of* (state specific purpose)." You may benefit by explaining more detail, such as the reason for choosing this form of servitor. For example;

"*I wish to create a servitor for the purpose of healing* (name person) *of the wasting disease of cancer. Let this spirit seek out and destroy the wasting cells, touching no others, and then return here to the flame of making that the servitor may be purified and returned to its element. Let it be so.*"

or;

"*I wish to create a servitor to guard this Temple by Fire. Let it watch and protect this place, bringing fear to the heart of any who shall intrude without my knowledge or consent, but let the servitor be bound by this token* (present sword or other implement to flames) *that this place shall be safe even from the Fire servitor's own consumptive nature. Let it be so.*"

These rituals can be elaborated on extensively, as other rituals can be created according to the needs of the situation. Only the guardian should be sustained, and that by repeated use or confirmation rituals if the Temple is not used frequently.

Notes About Candles

Candles are used in many rituals, if not as a focal point then at least as part of the Altar ornaments. Usually straight sided or votive candles are best. Decorative spiral candles are not recommended as spiral energies used in magic may be invoked by the shaping of these candles, and this is to be avoided unless one specifically wishes to conjure these energies.

DON'T FORGET GROUNDING!

One last time, I must emphasize the importance of grounding after a Fire ritual of any kind. There are very few exceptions to this. Residual Fire spirits have the potential to be a real menace. We have all seen the cartoons where little flames jump from one place to another, spontaneously multiplying and spreading the Fire as far as they can manage. This is a very good illustration of residual Fire energies out of control, but the Fire isn't always manifest in flame. The effects of other sorts of Fire spirits can be just as destructive in their own ways.

As I explained early in this book, they are not malicious any more than an animal which kills another animal for food is malicious. They do it because it is in their nature to do it. They are driven by the instinct to survive and to multiply, which are very strong drives in all of nature's beings. With appropriate regard for containment and grounding, no magician need ever fear the magic of the spirits of the Fire.

Bibliography

Aburrow, Yvonne. *The Enchanted Forest*. Berkshire: Capall Bann Publishing, 1993.

Arrowsmith, Nancy. *A Field Guide to the Little People*. London: MacMillan London Ltd., 1977.

Briggs, Katherine. *Abbey Lubbers, Banshees & Bogarts*. Harmondsworth: Kestrel Books, 1979.

Cavendish, Richard. *The Magical Arts*. London: Arkana Paperbacks, 1984.

Coghlan, Ronan. *Handbook of Fairies*. Berkshire: Capall Bann Publishing, 1998.

Cunningham, Scott. *Earth Power*. St. Paul, MN.: Llewellyn Publications, 1984.

Froud, Brian, Alan Lee. *Faeries*. New York: Bantam Books, 1978.

Hagger, Nicholas. *The Fire and the Stones*. Shaftesbury, Dorset: Element Books Ltd., 1991.

Jones, Evan John with Doreen Valiente. *Witchcraft: A Tradition Renewed*. Robert Hale Ltd., 1990.

Moore, A.W. *The Folk-Lore of the Isle of Man*. Felinfach: Llanerch Publishers,1994. (First published in 1891.)

Mullin, Kay. *Wondrous Land-The Faery Faith of Ireland*. Berkshire: Capall Bann Publishing, 1997.

Sepharial. *A Manual of Occultism*. London: Rider & Company, 1972.

Skelton, Robin. *Talismanic Magic*. York Beach, Maine: Samuel Weiser, Inc., 1985.

Spence, Lewis. *Myth and Ritual in Dance, Game and Rhyme*. London: Watts & Co., 1947.

Waite, Arthur Edward. *The Book of Ceremonial Magic*. London: Rider & Company, 1911.

Other Recommended Reading

Alexander, Marc. *British Folklore, Myths and Legends*. London: George Weidenfeld & Nicolson Ltd., 1982.

Briggs, Katherine M. *The Vanishing People*. London: B.T. Batsford Ltd., 1978.

De Valera, Sinead. *Fairy Tales of Ireland*. London: Four Square Books, 1967.

Evans-Wentz, W.Y. *The Fairy Faith in Celtic Countries*. New York: Citadel Press, 1990.

Foss, Michael. *Folktales of the British Isles*. London: GPS (Print) Ltd., 1977.

Gale, Jack. Goddesses, *Guardians & Groves-Awakening the Spirit of the Land*. Berkshire: Capall Bann Publishing, 1996.

Hestleton, Phillip. *Secret Places of the Goddess*. Berkshire: Capall Bann Publishing, 1996.

Spence, Lewis. *British Fairy Origins*. Wellingborough: The Aquarian Press, Ltd., 1946.

Index

adversary, 20
Aether, 6, 10, 65, 118
Ahura Mazda, 13
Air, 6, 9-10, 13, 17-19, 23, 25, 29-31, 43, 49, 57, 61, 64, 68-69, 86, 91, 95-96, 105, 116, 118, 123
alchemy, 19, 77, 79
anger, 19, 62, 67, 69, 81, 97, 103, 111
Animism, 76
Apollo, 37
athame, 66, 72, 74-75, 81, 111, 116-118
Austin Osman Spare, 33

Backdraft, 21, 27
banishing, 113-114, 124
BASILISC, 24
Bogomiles, 34

Caballah, 3, 7, 79, 81, 84
Chakras, 83
change, 13, 48, 54, 58, 61-62, 68, 78, 81, 88-89, 93-94, 112-113, 116
chaotic, 56, 63-64, 66, 81, 93, 96, 111
Corroboree, 39

death, 14, 18, 20, 26, 81, 90, 107, 109
Dervishes, 34
destruction, 15, 19-20, 25, 43, 48-49, 54, 105, 107
Devil Dancers, 34
Dion Fortune, 86
Dionysis, 37
Divine Fire, 13
Divine Light, 13, 109
Donald Michael Kraig, 122
Drachen, 25
dragons, 25
DRAKE, 25

Earth, 6, 9-10, 14, 17, 19, 21, 23, 26, 29, 39, 43-45, 48-49, 53-58, 64, 67, 69, 76, 79, 81, 89, 95-96, 104, 107, 127
ecstatic, 15, 17, 29-30, 34, 62, 76, 81, 99
Einstein, 33
essence, 29, 57-58, 73, 98, 120

faeryland, 34
fairies, 9-10, 14, 23, 33, 51, 58, 71-72, 127
fairy, 11, 21, 25, 33, 38, 40, 53, 128
Fates, 23

129

fear, 15, 19-20, 35, 45, 49, 55, 62-64, 78, 81, 87-88, 107, 125-126
FEE, 23
fertility, 14, 23, 35, 84, 102, 118, 120
FOLLETTI, 23
Frater U.D., 122

genie, 26
Gnosis, 109
Grak, 25
Great Serpent Mound, 26
guardian, 47, 73, 75, 94, 97, 112, 115, 125

Havelock Ellis, 33

incense, 7, 28, 57, 77, 84-86
Incubi, 26
incubus, 25
Isle of Man, 15, 71, 127

JINN, 26
jinnee, 26
Judith Lynne Hanna, Ph.D, 35

Khonds, 39
knot magic, 64
kundalini, 25-26, 30

La Brea tar pits, 45
Laa Lunys, 14
LAMIA, 25
life force, 13, 17, 19-20, 51, 56, 58, 79, 109

Loch Ness Monster, 26
Lucian, 37
Lugnassah, 14
lycanthropy, 81

masking, 37, 76
Midsummer, 14, 71
Mongolian Death Worm, 26
Morris dance, 39
Mount Olympus, 45

Needfire, 20
Nietzsche, 33
numbers, 87-88

Orgoi Horhoi, 27

passion, 13, 15, 17-20, 23, 29, 31, 33, 37, 43-44, 57-58, 61-62, 67, 69, 81, 93, 97, 103, 111, 115, 121
Peri Orcheseos, 37
Phoenix, 15, 19-20, 107
possessive spirits, 15, 29
primordial, 81
progression, 13, 61, 87, 94, 111-113
psychodrama, 67
purification, 15, 47-48, 61, 71, 77, 81, 84, 87, 118, 120

RARASH, 24
renewal, 49, 98, 102, 107
residual energies, 53, 76, 96, 112
Results, 15, 23, 79, 121
revenge, 25, 77, 94, 112-113

sacred woods, 84, 86
sacrifice, 15, 39, 44, 71
salamander, 24
Sephiroth, 79, 81, 83-84
serpent, 24, 26-27
servitor, 125
sex magic, 26, 119, 122
sex, 13, 15, 17, 25-26, 44, 57, 118-119, 122
shapeshifting, 76, 81
sigil, 68, 118-119
spiral, 26, 96, 126
Spirit, 7, 10, 13, 15, 17-20, 23-25, 27, 29-31, 33, 37, 40-41, 43-45, 47-49, 51-59, 61-62, 64, 66-69, 73-75, 77, 79, 81, 93, 95-99, 101-105, 109-110, 112-121, 124-125, 128
succubi, 26
succubus, 25, 27
Sun, 13-14, 20, 24, 39, 71, 85
sword, 39, 66, 72, 74, 81, 107, 111, 116-117, 125
sympathetic magic, 34, 37

Tantra, 26, 122
Temple, 26, 40, 73, 75, 77, 115-117, 125
The Dance, 15, 31, 33, 35, 37, 40, 43, 53-54, 56, 65, 101
The Exorcist, 29
Theseus, 37
Tibetan Book of the Dead, 14
transmutation, 13, 19-20, 79, 81, 86, 107, 116
Tuatha De Danaan, 21, 23
TYLWYTH TEG, 23, 40

Tylwyth Teg, 23, 40

underworld, 14-15, 18, 23-24, 66, 77

vacuity, 119
Verry Volk, 24
Volcano, 41, 45, 76, 81
VOUIVRE, 24

Wagner, 33
wand, 66, 72, 74-75, 81, 116-118
Water, 6, 9-10, 24, 26, 40, 49, 69, 77, 91, 99, 102, 122
Will, 9-10, 13, 15, 18-20, 23-24, 26-30, 41, 43, 47, 51-52, 56, 58, 61, 65-69, 75-76, 78, 81, 88, 93, 96-97, 101, 104-105, 107, 109-110, 112-113, 115-117, 119-124
William Shakespeare, 13, 31

Yeats, 33
Yule log, 66

The Fairies in the Irish Tradition by Molly Gowen

A comprehensive study of the fairy nature and its manifestations in the Irish tradition, illustrated with stories and legends and illuminated with superb artwork. Contents include: Fairy Nature - fallen angels, elementals and ghosts; Fairies in the Landscape; The Banshee; History of the Sidhe; the Fairy Doctor; Tir na nOg; magical animals, the Pooka, the King of Cats and Demon Dogs. Many superb illustrations by Lavinia Hamer. ISBN 186163 0859   £7.95

Handbook of Fairies by Ronan Coghlan

Many theories have been put forward about fairies - whether their origins are the deities of pre-Christian religions, primitive peoples driven into hiding, or even the denizens of UFOs. This is a detailed guide to fairies and other otherworldly beings. The different types of fairy and other otherworld beings are described, together with stories and legends, possible origins of fairies, links or differences from aliens, the passing of Otherworld time and other fascinating topics. . ISBN 186163 042 5   £9.95

Wondrous Land - The Faery Faith of Ireland by Kay Mullin

Dr Kay Mullin, a clinical psychologist by profession, was introduced to the world of faery by spirit channelled through a medium. That meeting led to extensive research in Ireland, collecting stories both old and new - from people who not only know of faeries, but see them too - in the land so long associated with them. The result is this wonderful book. The text is complemented with lyrical poetry from an Irish seer, and exquisite drawings. The faery faith is real, alive and growing in Ireland. Illustrated by Cormac Figgis. "....a delight...a living, personal story from the Atlantic edge..." 3rd Stone ISBN 186163 010 7   £10.95

Real Fairies by David Tame

Encounters with fairies seem to be increasing. This book relates the experiences of many people, some famous, some clairvoyant, some everyday, who have seen and met members of the fairy kingdom. It appears that our world and theirs are drawing closer together again and it is possible for more and more people to see what we have been told by some for generations does not exist. ISBN 186163 0719 £9.95

The Mythology of the Mermaid and Her Kin   by Marc Potts

Explores the origin of Mermaids and Mermen. Sea deities, especially those depicted as being fish-tailed are explored, as is the mythology of woman's association with water. The folklore of mermaids is related, especially from Britain and Northern Europe, with relevant examples from other parts of the world. Other topics related include: the mermaid's image in bestiaries, the mermaid and the Christian church, carvings and heraldry, recorded sightings and captures, the seal/siren explanation, mermaid hoaxes and the mermaids' image today. The text is illustrated by Marc's superb paintings. ISBN 18663 0395

FREE DETAILED CATALOGUE

Capall Bann is owned and run by people actively involved in many of the areas in which we publish. A detailed illustrated catalogue is available on request, SAE or International Postal Coupon appreciated. **Titles can be ordered direct from Capall Bann, post free in the UK** (cheque or PO with order) or from good bookshops and specialist outlets. Do contact us for details on the latest releases at: **Capall Bann Publishing, Freshfields, Chieveley, Berks, RG20 8TF.** Titles include:

A Breath Behind Time, Terri Hector
Angels and Goddesses - Celtic Christianity & Paganism, M. Howard
Arthur - The Legend Unveiled, C Johnson & E Lung
Astrology The Inner Eye - A Guide in Everyday Language, E Smith
Auguries and Omens - The Magical Lore of Birds, Yvonne Aburrow
Asyniur - Womens Mysteries in the Northern Tradition, S McGrath
Begonnings - Geomancy, Builder's Rites & Electional Astrology in the European Tradition, Nigel Pennick
Between Earth and Sky, Julia Day
Book of the Veil , Peter Paddon
Caer Sidhe - Celtic Astrology and Astronomy, Vol 1, Michael Bayley
Caer Sidhe - Celtic Astrology and Astronomy, Vol 2 M Bayley
Call of the Horned Piper, Nigel Jackson
Cat's Company, Ann Walker
Celtic Faery Shamanism, Catrin James
Celtic Faery Shamanism - The Wisdom of the Otherworld, Catrin James
Celtic Lore & Druidic Ritual, Rhiannon Ryall
Celtic Sacifice - Pre Christian Ritual & Religion, Marion Pearce
Celtic Saints and the Glastonbury Zodiac, Mary Caine
Circle and the Square, Jack Gale
Compleat Vampyre - The Vampyre Shaman, Nigel Jackson
Creating Form From the Mist - The Wisdom of Women in Celtic Myth and Culture, Lynne Sinclair-Wood
Crystal Clear - A Guide to Quartz Crystal, Jennifer Dent
Crystal Doorways, Simon & Sue Lilly
Crossing the Borderlines - Guising, Masking & Ritual Animal Disguise in the European Tradition, Nigel Pennick
Dragons of the West, Nigel Pennick
Earth Dance - A Year of Pagan Rituals, Jan Brodie

Earth Harmony - Places of Power, Holiness & Healing, Nigel Pennick
Earth Magic, Margaret McArthur
Eildon Tree (The) Romany Language & Lore, Michael Hoadley
Enchanted Forest - The Magical Lore of Trees, Yvonne Aburrow
Eternal Priestess, Sage Weston
Eternally Yours Faithfully, Roy Radford & Evelyn Gregory
Everything You Always Wanted To Know About Your Body, But So Far Nobody's Been Able To Tell You, Chris Thomas & D Baker
Face of the Deep - Healing Body & Soul, Penny Allen
Fairies in the Irish Tradition, Molly Gowen
Familiars - Animal Powers of Britain, Anna Franklin
Fool's First Steps, (The) Chris Thomas
Forest Paths - Tree Divination, Brian Harrison, Ill. S. Rouse
From Past to Future Life, Dr Roger Webber
God Year, The, Nigel Pennick & Helen Field
Goddess on the Cross, Dr George Young
Goddess Year, The, Nigel Pennick & Helen Field
Goddesses, Guardians & Groves, Jack Gale
Handbook For Pagan Healers, Liz Joan
Handbook of Fairies, Ronan Coghlan
Healing Book, The, Chris Thomas and Diane Baker
Healing Homes, Jennifer Dent
Healing Journeys, Paul Williamson
Healing Stones, Sue Philips
Herb Craft - Shamanic & Ritual Use of Herbs, Lavender & Franklin
Hidden Heritage - Exploring Ancient Essex, Terry Johnson
Hub of the Wheel, Skytoucher
In Search of Herne the Hunter, Eric Fitch
Inner Celtia, Alan Richardson & David Annwn
Inner Mysteries of the Goths, Nigel Pennick
Inner Space Workbook - Develop Thru Tarot, C Summers & J Vayne
Intuitive Journey, Ann Walker Isis - African Queen, Akkadia Ford
Journey Home, The, Chris Thomas
Kecks, Keddles & Kesh - Celtic Lang & The Cog Almanac, Bayley
Language of the Psycards, Berenice
Legend of Robin Hood, The, Richard Rutherford-Moore
Lid Off the Cauldron, Patricia Crowther
Light From the Shadows - Modern Traditional Witchcraft, Gwyn
Living Tarot, Ann Walker
Lore of the Sacred Horse, Marion Davies
Lost Lands & Sunken Cities (2nd ed.), Nigel Pennick
Magic of Herbs - A Complete Home Herbal, Rhiannon Ryall
Magical Guardians - Exploring the Spirit and Nature of Trees, Philip Heselton

Magical History of the Horse, Janet Farrar & Virginia Russell
Magical Lore of Animals, Yvonne Aburrow
Magical Lore of Cats, Marion Davies
Magical Lore of Herbs, Marion Davies
Magick Without Peers, Ariadne Rainbird & David Rankine
Masks of Misrule - Horned God & His Cult in Europe, Nigel Jackson
Medicine For The Coming Age, Lisa Sand MD
Medium Rare - Reminiscences of a Clairvoyant, Muriel Renard
Menopause and the Emotions, Kathleen I Macpherson
Mind Massage - 60 Creative Visualisations, Marlene Maundrill
Mirrors of Magic - Evoking the Spirit of the Dewponds, P Heselton
Moon Mysteries, Jan Brodie
Mysteries of the Runes, Michael Howard
Mystic Life of Animals, Ann Walker
New Celtic Oracle The, Nigel Pennick & Nigel Jackson
Oracle of Geomancy, Nigel Pennick
Pagan Feasts - Seasonal Food for the 8 Festivals, Franklin & Phillips
Patchwork of Magic - Living in a Pagan World, Julia Day
Pathworking - A Practical Book of Guided Meditations, Pete Jennings
Personal Power, Anna Franklin
Pickingill Papers - The Origins of Gardnerian Wicca, Bill Liddell
Pillars of Tubal Cain, Nigel Jackson
Places of Pilgrimage and Healing, Adrian Cooper
Practical Divining, Richard Foord
Practical Meditation, Steve Hounsome
Practical Spirituality, Steve Hounsome
Psychic Self Defence - Real Solutions, Jan Brodie
Real Fairies, David Tame
Reality - How It Works & Why It Mostly Doesn't, Rik Dent
Romany Tapestry, Michael Houghton
Runic Astrology, Nigel Pennick
Sacred Animals, Gordon MacLellan
Sacred Celtic Animals, Marion Davies, Ill. Simon Rouse
Sacred Dorset - On the Path of the Dragon, Peter Knight
Sacred Grove - The Mysteries of the Forest, Yvonne Aburrow
Sacred Geometry, Nigel Pennick
Sacred Nature, Ancient Wisdom & Modern Meanings, A Cooper
Sacred Ring - Pagan Origins of British Folk Festivals, M. Howard
Season of Sorcery - On Becoming a Wisewoman, Poppy Palin
Seasonal Magic - Diary of a Village Witch, Paddy Slade
Secret Places of the Goddess, Philip Heselton
Secret Signs & Sigils, Nigel Pennick
Self Enlightenment, Mayan O'Brien

Spirits of the Air, Jaq D Hawkins
Spirits of the Earth, Jaq D Hawkins
Spirits of the Earth, Jaq D Hawkins
Stony Gaze, Investigating Celtic Heads John Billingsley
Stumbling Through the Undergrowth , Mark Kirwan-Heyhoe
Subterranean Kingdom, The, revised 2nd ed, Nigel Pennick
Symbols of Ancient Gods, Rhiannon Ryall
Talking to the Earth, Gordon MacLellan
Taming the Wolf - Full Moon Meditations, Steve Hounsome
Teachings of the Wisewomen, Rhiannon Ryall
The Other Kingdoms Speak, Helena Hawley
Tree: Essence of Healing, Simon & Sue Lilly
Tree: Essence, Spirit & Teacher, Simon & Sue Lilly
Through the Veil, Peter Paddon
Torch and the Spear, Patrick Regan
Understanding Chaos Magic, Jaq D Hawkins
Vortex - The End of History, Mary Russell
Warp and Weft - In Search of the I-Ching, William de Fancourt
Warriors at the Edge of Time, Jan Fry
Water Witches, Tony Steele
Way of the Magus, Michael Howard
Weaving a Web of Magic, Rhiannon Ryall
West Country Wicca, Rhiannon Ryall
Wildwitch - The Craft of the Natural Psychic, Poppy Palin
Wildwood King , Philip Kane
Witches of Oz, Matthew & Julia Philips
Wondrous Land - The Faery Faith of Ireland by Dr Kay Mullin
Working With the Merlin, Geoff Hughes
Your Talking Pet, Ann Walker
Menopausal Woman on the Run, Jaki da Costa
Environmenta
Gardening For Wildlife Ron Wilson

FREE detailed catalogue and FREE 'Inspiration' magazine
Contact: Capall Bann Publishing, Freshfields, Chieveley, Berks, RG20 8TF